Healing
Jewelry

NO LONGER PROPERTY OF
SEATTLE PUBLIC LIBRARY

Healing
Jewelry

Mickey Baskett

Sterling Publishing Co., Inc.
New York

Prolific Impressions Production Staff:

Editor in Chief: Mickey Baskett
Copy Editor: Phyllis Mueller
Graphics: Dianne Miller, Karen Turpin
Styling: Lenos Key
Photography: Jerry Mucklow
Administration: Jim Baskett

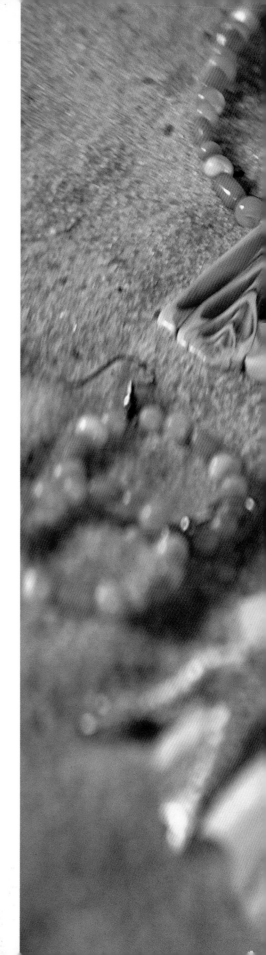

Every effort has been made to insure that the information presented is accurate. Since we have no control over physical conditions, individual skills, or chosen tools and products, the publisher disclaims any liability for injuries, losses, untoward results, or any other damages which may result from the use of the information in this book. Thoroughly read the instructions for all products used to complete the projects in this book, paying particular attention to all cautions and warnings shown for that product to ensure their proper and safe use.

No part of this book may be reproduced for commercial purposes in any form without permission by the copyright holder. The written instructions and design patterns in this book are intended for the personal use of the reader and may be reproduced for that purpose only.

Library of Congress Cataloging-in-Publication Data

Baskett, Mickey.
  Healing jewelry / Mickey Baskett.
      p. cm.
  Includes index.
  ISBN-13: 978-1-4027-3518-9
  ISBN-10: 1-4027-3518-9
  1. Precious stones--Therapeutic use. 2. Jewelry--Therapeutic use. I. Title.
RZ560.B37 2007
615.8'515--dc22

                                                    2006032788

2   4   6   8   10   9   7   5   3   1

Published by Sterling Publishing Co., Inc.
387 Park Avenue South, New York, NY 10016
© 2007 by Prolific Impressions, Inc.
Distributed in Canada by Sterling Publishing
c/o Canadian Manda Group, 165 Dufferin Street,
Toronto, Ontario, Canada M6K 3H6
Distributed in the United Kingdom by GMC Distribution Services,
Castle Place, 166 High Street, Lewes, East Sussex, England BN7 1XU
Distributed in Australia by Capricorn Link (Australia) Pty. Ltd.
P.O. Box 704, Windsor, NSW 2756, Australia

Printed in China

All rights reserved

ISBN 13: 978-1-4027-3518-9
ISBN 10: 1-4027-3518-9

For information about custom editions, special sales, premium and corporate purchases, please contact Sterling Special Sales Department at 800-805-5489 or specialsales@sterlingpub.com.

PAGE 26

PAGE 41

Contents

PAGE 56

PAGE 77

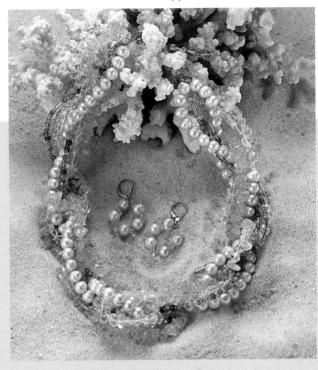

Balancing Aesthetics & Spirituality

There's no denying gemstones are beautiful to see and sensuous to touch. Who can resist the sparkle of amethyst, the earthy warmth of jade and turquoise, the luminosity of pearls, or the glow of amber? Semi-precious stones and beads have been used for centuries as jewelry and adornment. They also have a long history as talis-

This book provides information about the believed healing powers of a variety of gemstones as well as the history and folklore surrounding those stones. Also included in this book are more than 50 projects featuring these gemstones. You can learn how to craft beautiful jewelry pieces and traditional devotional items like rosaries, prayer beads, and malas. Detailed supply lists, instruc-

Gemstones are believed to possess powerful healing properties.

mans, amulets, and ritual objects because they are believed to possess powerful healing characteristics and to produce particular spiritual effects.

It's possible that you're sensing their power to affect you when you're drawn, for example, to choose a jade necklace instead of a peridot one on a particular day (after all, they're both green). Or when a turquoise bracelet, all of a sudden, is something you want to have on your wrist day after day. Or when you're willing to (irrationally, it might seem) spend twenty minutes looking for your pearl earrings because you don't feel like you can leave the house without them. Or it may be nothing at all.

tions, and patterns will guide you along the way. You'll find one-of-kind ideas for using a single type of gemstone bead like the Garnet Scallops Necklace as well as pieces that use interesting combinations of colors, textures, and sheens of stones with glass, wood, and metal beads and charms of various types.

I hope you enjoy exploring the spiritual qualities and mythical meanings of beads and stones and that you create jewelry you enjoy wearing and giving.

Mickey Baskett

Stones have been used as talismans.

BEADING SUPPLIES

This section provides information about supplies you'll need for jewelry making - beads, wire and thread for stringing, jewelry findings, glues, and tools. Beading supplies are available at bead stores, stores that sell supplies for making jewelry, craft outlets, and on the Internet.

Gemstones

Natural gemstones are the focal point of the jewelry pieces in this book. You'll find a wide variety of shapes, cuts, and sizes of stones available at bead and craft stores as well as online, including carved shapes, chips, coin shapes, cubes, drops, ovals, rounds, nuggets, pillow cuts, rice cuts, and both faceted and round finishes. The fun part is picking out the stones that capture your fancy, the ones that "speak to you," so to speak. Most gemstones and beads are sized in millimeters (mm).

Words Used to Describe Gemstones & Beads

Opaque: No light can pass through. Examples: Pearl, turquoise, hematite, lapis, malachite.
Translucent: Somewhat clear, light can pass through. Examples: Crystal, ruby, sapphire, emerald .
Iris: An iridescent coating, usually on dark, opaque beads.
AB (Aurora Borealis): A pastel multi-colored coating on translucent beads.
Matte: Not shiny. Matte glass beads usually have been chemically etched and have a frosted look.
Ghost: Translucent matte beads with an AB coating.

Seed Beads

Using seed beads in jewelry pieces fills space and adds interest and color. Seed beads are small, rounded glass beads. They may be categorized as oblate (i.e., they are fatter in diameter than they are long) or cylinder (as long or longer than they are fat).

Seed beads are sized in aughts, which are different from millimeters. One version of seed bead sizing lists the size as the number of seed beads in an inch (example: 11/0, eleven beads to the inch). The important thing to remember is that bead sizes are in inverse proportion to the size of the bead. Size 24 is tiny, and size 5 is big.

Rocaille-type seed beads are silver- (or gold-) lined beads with square holes. The term **charlotte** is used to describe size 13 seed beads that have one hand-cut side on each bead. This makes them slightly faceted. An **E bead** is also a seed bead, but is larger (size 4, 5, or 6). An exterior metallic coating is sometimes added to seed beads - these beads are called **AB beads**. (AB means "Aurora Borealis.")

Buying seed beads: Seed beads are sold in a variety of containers, from small packets and bags to large tubes, tiny blister packs to hanks (beads on temporary string carriers), and sometimes measured by weight in grams. Hanks of (usually) 12 strands contain larger quantities and are often the most economically priced.

Variety Beads

There is an almost endless variety of beads you can use along with your gemstones. Beads are made all over the world of glass, wood, ceramic, metal, acrylic, clay, and natural minerals. They are classified according to their material, shape, and size. Most beads have holes for stringing. Their sizes are usually measured in millimeters (mm).

Beading Wire, Thread & Cord

BEAD STRINGING WIRE

Jewelry stringing wire is made by a variety of manufacturers and may have different names. It's made of woven strands of stainless steel wire that are coated in nylon so beading wire is waterproof (it won't rust or tarnish), flexible, and hypoallergenic. It comes in colors to coordinate with beads.

Wire comes in different diameters - the thicker the wire, the better its resistance to breaking and cutting. Choose the diameter that best fits the beads you plan to use. For pearls or seed beads, use a small diameter wire. A medium diameter will work for almost any jewelry project. Larger diameter wire is designed for items such as bracelets and watches that must withstand a lot of movement and bumping.

Tigertail is a type of beading wire that is one of the easiest stringing materials to use. It is plastic coated and doesn't need a needle for stringing; the ends are easy to finish with crimp beads. However, tigertail kinks easily and is weakened where it has kinked.

Flex wire can be knotted and will not kink. It is very strong and comes in various colors and sizes. It is great for all types of beads because of its strength and flexibility.

BEADING THREAD

Beading thread is usually made of nylon and is very strong. Thread requires a needle and is commonly used with beading needles. Because it's very thin, beading thread can go through most beads multiple times, or the thread can be doubled to make it thicker and stronger. **Beeswax** can be used to coat it - this conditions it and keeps it from tangling and protects from fraying when it is repeatedly passed through the sharp edges of the holes in tiny beads. The finest thread is sized 00 and goes up in size from there: size 0, then sizes A through F.

WAXED NYLON

Waxed nylon is a braided bead thread. It's just stiff enough that, for general bead stringing, you don't need a needle! It also knots very nicely.

Pictured above, clockwise from bottom left: Beading wire, dark beading thread, needles, beading thread, wax.

WAXED LINEN

This works well with most beads, but it's a little too large to fit through many seed and bugle beads. It knots and braids well and is excellent for necklaces that have beads up to the clasp.

LEATHER CORD

This is very easy to work with and is nice to use when stringing an interesting pendant. When using leather cord, tie knots to hold the beads in place. Add a clasp or make the necklace long enough to go over the head. Black, dark brown, and natural colors are the most popular.

RATTAIL CORD

This round, satin-finish fiber cord is often used to show off one large centerpiece stone or bead. Since rough or thin edges can fray this cord, it's a good idea to use necklace tubes rather than jump rings on the backs of pendants. Single strands are usually finished with fold-over crimps, and multiple strands with bullet ends.

Continued on next page

Beading Wire, Thread & Cord continued from page 11

ELASTIC CORD or STRETCH NYLON

This is most often used for snug-fitting bracelets and necklaces. It's a good choice if the wearer's coordination might be a problem (it's great for kids' jewelry!). For durability, use the heaviest cord that will work with your beads. Finish with square knots.

BEADING NEEDLES

When using thin beading thread or cord, rather than wire, you will need a beading needle for stringing the beads. Needles come in different sizes; choose a needle that will fit through the holes of the beads you plan to use.

Beading needles come in regulars and sharps. Sharps are not any sharper than other needles, but they are shorter and usually stiffer. Personal preference is usually the reason for choosing a regular beading needle or a sharp.

BEADING NEEDLES	
Bead Size	Needle Size
10 or larger	Size 10
11 and 12	Size 12
13 and 14	Size 13
15 and smaller	Size 15

BEADING FOUNDATION

Stiff, stabilizing fabric used on the back of beaded brooches. The fabric is cut into shapes and beads are sewn to it.

Jewelry Findings

Jewelry findings are the metal items that transform beads and wire and thread into jewelry. You will need the following:

Clasps: These come in a wide variety of shapes, sizes, and designs. Some are ornate, and some are plain. Some are meant to be seen; others are meant to be overlooked. There are *barrel clasps, spring lock clasps, lobster clasps, toggle clasps, fishhook clasps,* and *box clasps. Magnetic clasps* contain tiny magnets that hold them together. The individual project instructions specify the type of clasp used, but the final choice is up to you.

Jump rings or **split rings** are small metal rings that are used to attach one finding to another (for example, an eye pin to an earring wire) or to attach a strand of beads to a finding. They are split and can be pried open for use. Split rings are usually more secure than a jump ring.

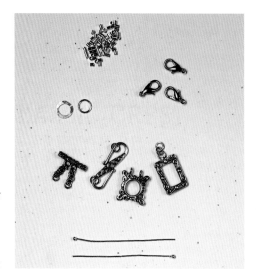

Earring findings come in unpierced and pierced varieties. **Pierced backs** fall into three categories: hooks, posts, and chains. **Unpierced backs** are available as screw-on or clip-on.

Pin backs and stick pins are sewn or glued to transform a jewelry design into a pin.

Head pins and eye pins are used to construct drop earrings and dangles. They come in a variety of lengths, metals, and finishes. A head pin looks like a straight pin without a pointed end. An eye pin has a loop on one end.

Crimp beads are used to secure strands of beads to findings and lengths of chain or to permanently join the ends of a necklace meant to be slipped over the head. They are made of very soft metal, and when squeezed with a crimping tool they are permanently shut. You will need to match the diameter of your crimp beads (also called "crimp tubes") to the diameter of the wire. If you use a heavy wire, a larger diameter crimp bead will be needed.

Adhesives

Occasionally, beads or stones are secured with glue. When choosing glue, read the label carefully and choose one to work with the materials you are using. **Beading glue** is strong and flexible. Use it for securing knotted threads. **One-part epoxy adhesive** and **clear cement** are good choices for attaching stones.

Tools

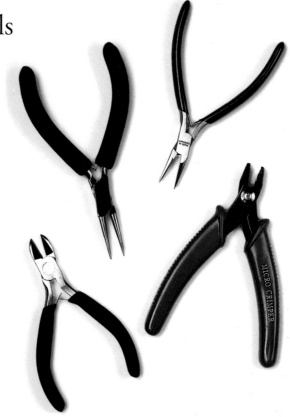

Having the right tool is important and makes any task easier and more pleasurable. Choose pliers and cutters with spring-loaded handles; they are much easier on your hands.

Wire cutters have handles like pliers and sharp blades for cutting wire. *Always* cut wire with wire cutters - *never* use scissors.

Side cutters are sharp wire cutters that are designed for close cutting - they don't leave sharp wire ends that will poke you when you wear your jewelry.

Roundnose pliers have smooth, round, tapered jaws. They are essential for making smooth wire wraps for dangles.

Needlenose pliers with flat inner surfaces and pointed ends are great for flattening and getting into small spaces.

Chain-nose pliers have flat jaws and are used to grab and flatten. The best chain-nose pliers for making jewelry are smooth. Pliers with grippers might seem helpful, but they're not - they mar the wire.

Pictured above, clockwise from top left: roundnose pliers, chain nose pliers, crimping tool, side cutters.

Crimping tool (also called "crimping pliers") has two holes on the jaw. Use it to close crimp beads and crimp tubes.

Beading board will give you a surface for holding your beads in compartments and is helpful when designing and stringing beads. Many boards have measurements on them also.

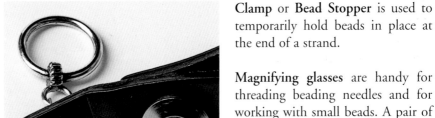

Above: Crimping tool

Clamp or **Bead Stopper** is used to temporarily hold beads in place at the end of a strand.

Magnifying glasses are handy for threading beading needles and for working with small beads. A pair of good-quality **Tweezers** is helpful for picking up beads and untangling threads.

Scissors are needed for cutting thread - but don't use them on wire.

FINISHING ENDS
Using Bead Tips

With this technique, a clamp shell bead tip is used to hide the knot in beading thread and for holding the clasp. This technique is recommended for necklaces and not bracelets because the bead tip is flexible and can come off with wear and tear.

You will need: 2 clam shell bead tips, beading thread or cord, clear jewelry cement, chain nose pliers

1. Tie a knot in the end of the beading thread that is larger than the hole in the bead tip. Pull the other end of the thread through the hole in the bead tip so that the knot is in the bead tip. Trim the excess thread and dab the knot with cement.
2. Using the pliers, press the bead tip closed.
3. Before using the pliers to press the loop closed, add your clasp.

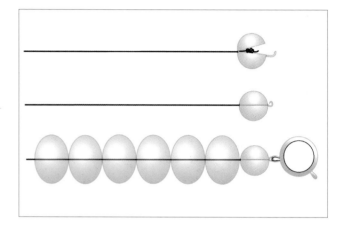

4. Add beads and finish the other end in the same way. Pull the thread through the bead tip before tying the knot.

Bullet Ends

Use this type of end when stringing with wire.

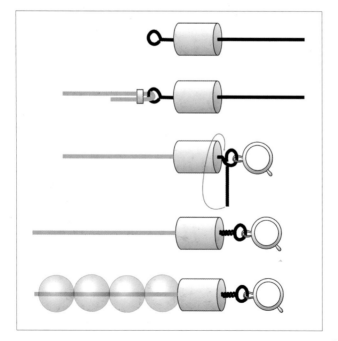

End Caps

For fine jewelry, use silver-plated sterling end caps. These are used to hold the ends of leather, rubber or thicker fabric cords. Add a drop of clear jewelry cement to the cord end and push into the end cap.

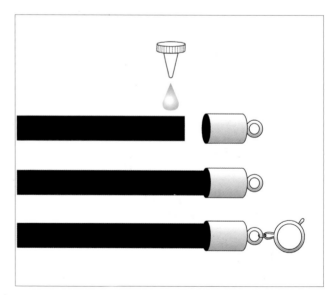

Crimp Beads

1. Use this technique when working with beading wire. Thread a crimp bead on the end of beading wire. Thread the wire through the clasp, then back through the crimp bead. Leave a 1" tail. Crimp the bead with flat nosed pliers.
2. Thread beads on the wire and over the wire tail.
3. At the necklace end, thread a crimp bead on wire. Thread the wire through the other end of the clasps, then back through the crimp bead and several beads. Pull wire taut. Crimp bead. Cut wire tail.

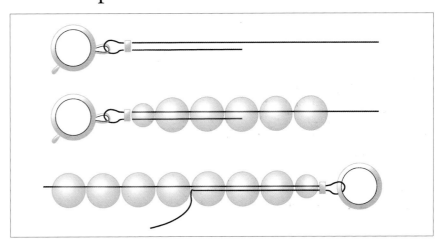

Fold-Over Crimps

This finding end has an attached ring for a clasp. This type of crimp end is best for use with cording.

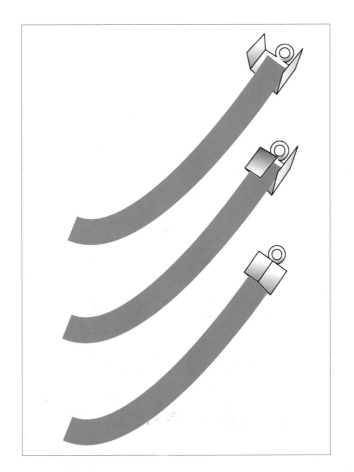

Knots

Use these types of knots with beading thread to secure ends.

Square Knot

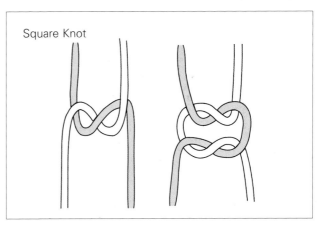

Double Loop Knot or Figure-8 Knot

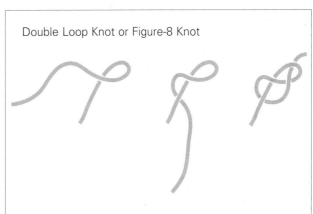

Healing Properties of Stones

In this section you'll find information we've gathered about the purported properties of gemstones used to make the jewelry in this book, including history, legends, folklore, and myths. Use it for your own education, as a jumping-off point for doing your own research, as a guide to using and wearing gemstones, or merely as entertainment.

But do be aware that some alternative healers and New Age believers view crystal and gem healing as an art and practice on a metaphysical level. They have rediscovered ancient uses for gemstones and use them in healing many different types of ailments, believing the vital power of the earth's energies has been absorbed by the stones, giving them distinctive physical and spiritual characteristics.

Healing practices that use gemstones include chakra healing, psychic healing, Eastern medicine, purification rituals, Vedic astrology, and followers of Atlantis religion, the occult, paranormal psychology, aromatherapy, metaphysics, and ESP.

16

Abalone

Color & Physical Properties:
Abalone is a shell that has an oval shape and an iridescent interior. The interior sheen includes many colors of the rainbow. It can be found in South America and Asia.

Healing Properties:
Enlivens the body.
Native northwest Native Americans used the shells as a vessel for cleansing, and for offerings.

Agate

Color & Physical Properties:
Agates are aggregates of various forms of silica. Agates are found in shades of red, yellow, brown, orange, black, and white.

Healing Properties:
Strengthen a person's connection to the earth by grounding the emotions. Lessens feelings of envy. In particular, crazy lace agates relieve emotional pain, improve stamina, and ward off evil. Multicolored agates will give you strength for carrying out your goals.

Amazonite

Color & Physical Properties:
A variety of feldspar, amazonite is a semi-opaque stone and is usually polished in the form of a cabochon. It can be bright verdigris green to bluish green. It was once believed to be jade. Was used extensively by early Egyptians and was called the stone of courage.

Healing Properties:
Improve confidence.
Restores spiritual faith.
Enhances creative expression and self-worth.
A good stone for writers and other creative people.

Amber

Color & Physical Properties:
Amber is a petrified resin from ancient pine trees. Amber's colorings range from a deep brown to an almost clear lemon yellow. Amber is often labeled by its area of origin, e.g., **Baltic amber** is from eastern Europe.

Healing Properties:
Electromagnetic in nature - helps the body heal itself.
Transforms negative energy into positive energy.
It helps to calm the nerves and enliven the disposition.
It can add stability and bring about a positive state of mind.
Purifies the body, mind, and spirit.

Amethyst

Color & Physical Properties:
Amethyst is a purple variety of quartz and the birthstone for people born in February. It is the most valued stone of the quartz family. The stone must be purple to be an amethyst, but it can come in a variety of shades of purple. Purple is the color of royalty, so amethysts were used in the ancient ornaments of Greeks and Egyptians. The British crown jewels also contain amethysts.

Healing Properties:
Stone of meditation and spirituality. Cleanses, purifies, restructures, and renews. Reduces anger, impatience, and nightmares. It can also help to overcome addictions. The ancient Greeks believed people who wore an amethyst or drank from an amethyst chalice would not become intoxicated.

Aventurine

Color & Physical Properties:
Aventurine is a variety of micro-crystalline quartz. It can be translucent to opaque and have inclusions of shiny minerals such as mica. There is a wide range of colors - green, peach, brown, blue. It is often mistaken for jade or amazonite.

Healing Properties:
Heals the heart by releasing emotional stress.
Allows reuniting of the healthy heart and soul.
Heal emotional pain, fear, negativity and imbalance.
Calm a troubled spirit and brings about inner peace.
It is often used as a lucky stone. It was used in the Native American Medicine Wheel rituals. When held over the heart of the participants, they felt a wave of love all around them.

Calcite

Color & Physical Properties:
It is an abundant crystal that can be white, gray, black, green, yellow, brown, or blue.

Healing Properties:
Sharpens mental clarity. Boosts memory. It is uplifting, bringing joy, happiness, and humor. Improves relationship with and understanding of nature.

Carnelian

Color & Physical Properties:
This stone is a form of chalcedony, a member of the quartz family. It ranges in color from deep red to orange. It is one of the oldest stones used in jewelry making - found in Egyptian tombs.

Healing Properties:
Represents the fertility of the earth.
Signifies strength.
Reinforces confidence, initiative, dramatic abilities, and assertiveness. A stone of passion and sexuality. Protects against anger and fear. Improves sense of touch.

Cat's Eye

Color & Physical Properties:
It can be translucent gold or green or clear green or brown. It is rarer than tiger's eye, but often mistaken for it.

Healing Properties:
Promotes prosperity. Confidence.

Citrine

Color & Physical Properties:
Transparent sunshine yellow. Its name comes from the same root as *citron,* the French word for lemon.

Healing Properties:
Promotes a bright, happy disposition. Increases physical and material power. Expands mental clarity.

Coral

Color & Physical Properties:
Made up of calcium and calcite. Coral is the hard stony skeleton of a sea creature. Coral may be red, salmon, or pink in color, and its color is uniform throughout.

Healing Properties:
Quiets the emotions, bringing peace. Can facilitate intuition, imagination, and visualization. Calming. Recommended for brides.

Crystals, Quartz

Color & Physical Properties:
Clear crystals known as crystal quartz or rock crystals are one of earth's most common minerals. Quartz encompasses a large family of stones and crystals, all of which are made up of silicon dioxide, one of the most common substances in the world. Crystals of pure quartz, which are generally six-sided, can be found in all shades and colors.

Healing Properties:
Crystals are used for harmony. One of the most powerful healers. Crystals are used for meditation, transformation, protection, and enlightenment. They promote general good health and balance.

Fluorite

Color & Physical Properties:
Comes in all colors - deep purple,(its most famous) amethyst, sky blue, sea green, sunny yellow, and crystal clear. There are rarer colors of pink, reddish orange (rose) and even black. Has a crystal structure. Fluorite is a beautiful and interesting mineral, and very popular among mineral collectors.

Healing Properties:
Increases the life force and expands mental power. Clears the mind of stress. Enhances serenity and strengthens consciousness.

Garnet

Color & Physical Properties:
Garnet is the January birthstone. Most often recognized as a deep red, but can range in color from deep emerald green through yellow, brown, and red. Many varieties of garnets are named for their color. It is common to the United States, but found all over the world. Garnets are formed under high pressure and/or high temperature. The name is believed to be derived from the word "pomegranate" because of its resemblance to the jewel-like fruit.

Healing Properties:
Stimulates creativity, passion.
Garnet is useful in avoiding bad dreams.
Garnets were once exchanged as gifts between friends to demonstrate their affection for one other and to insure meeting again.
Helps calm anger.

Hematite

Color & Physical Properties:
Hematite (iron ore) is a very common mineral on Earth. It is most often a silver-gray metallic, but can be found in rainbow varieties. Found in the US, Brazil, and Canada. Hematite is derived from the Greek word meaning "blood". In soft powder form, it is called "red ocher".

Healing Properties:
A protective stone.
Helps bolster low self-esteem.
Hematite is known to deflect negativity.
It restores equilibrium, and stability.
Helps concentration and memory.

Jade

Color & Physical Properties:
The most valuable form of jade is known as imperial jade and is an emerald green color. Jades also appear in mottled green and white. The range of greens are light to dark, creamy, and grayish. Because it has a smooth even texture, it has been a preferred material for carving and for jewelry, where it is cut into cabochons.

Healing Properties:
A powerful emotional balancer. Brings peace, wisdom, courage, and clarity. Radiates divine, unconditional love. Increase longevity. Jade is the stone of health, wealth, and long life. For almost a thousand years, jade has been worshiped for its life-extending powers. Brings good luck and fortune.

Jasper

Color & Physical Properties:
It is an opaque and fine-grained variety of chalcedony. It can be found in all colors. Many times it will have patterns or bands of colors from inclusions of organic material and/or mineral oxides. Picture jasper gets its name from its patterns that look like landscapes, containing hills and valleys.

Healing Properties:
Each color of jasper has specific qualities.
Overall, believed to stabilize emotions and reduce fears.
Yellow jasper stimulates the heart area and nurtures the digestive organs.
Red jasper is used for bronchial problems and to strengthen the blood.
Brown - grounding.
Green - overall healing.
Poppy jasper enhances organizational abilities, relaxation, and a sense of wholeness.
Picture jasper encourages creativity.
Leopard skin jasper stabilizes frustrations, bringing serenity and mental clarity.
Gray - serenity; black - protection; pink - love.

continued from page 19

Labradorite

Color & Physical Properties:
A feldspar stone. The name is derived from Labrador, the original source of the Canadian variety of this stone. It is highly iridescent and vividly colored.

Healing Properties:
An excellent stone for blind people - helps gauge distance. Brings forth each person's strengths. Help us to relate to others.

Lapis Lazuli

Color & Physical Properties:
It is one of the most valuable semi-opaque stones. It is most often a solid strong blue. But is most valuable when it is found with small veins of pyrite. Lapis was used extensively in ancient Egypt and has been mined in Afghanistan for over 7,000 years. The ancient city of Ur had a thriving trade in lapis as early as the 4th century BC.

Healing Properties:
Organizes and quiets the mind, as well as adding wisdom. Helps heal anxiety, restlessness, insomnia, and depressions.Protects from physical harm. Points the way to enlightenment.

Malachite

Color & Physical Properties:
An opaque stone with bands of deep green to black/green. It has a high copper content and is a copper carbonate.

Healing Properties:
Improve mental strength. Stabilizes the psyche. Used for protection, peace, and success in business. A guardian stone for travelers.

Mariposite

Color & Physical Properties:
An attractive translucent green color. It is a marble variety containing mica and varying amounts of quartz and dolomite. When used for jewelry the stone is sometimes called emerald quartz. *Mariposa* is the Spanish word for butterfly.

Healing Properties:
Mariposite is the power stone for artists. Stimulate self-expression and creativity. Help one adapt easily and successfully to new situations.

Moonstone

Color & Physical Properties:
This stone belongs to the feldspar family. It is opalescent and can range from colorless to blue, green, peach. Moonstone has been found in ancient Roman jewelry where it was believed to have been formed from the light of the moon.

Healing Properties:
Soothes stress and anxiety. Balances emotions. It calms the emotions and cures headaches.

Mother of Pearl

Color & Physical Properties:
Mother of pearl isn't a stone, but comes from the lining of pearl oyster seashells. It is listed her with other healing stones because it is used widely in jewelry making and it also contains healing powers.

Healing Properties:
As the sea calms and relieves stress, mother of pearl carries this same energy. Wear mother of pearl for relaxation and soothing of emotions.

Onyx

Color & Physical Properties:
It is a form of quartz. It is fine-textured and usually black. However some can be found with white bands, which is sometimes called sardonyx.

Healing Properties:
This stone protects against negativity. Balances the physical being and strengthens the mind. It can be used to banish grief, enhance self control, and encourage wise decision-making. It increases happiness and good fortune.

Pearl

Color & Physical Properties:
Pearl is the June birthstone. It is usually white or cream colored, but black, blue and gray varieties can be found. The pearl's luster comes from the unique way it reflects light—light rays reflect off both the surface of the pearl and also off the concentric inner layers of nacre. Nacre is a lustrous substance that coats irritants such as sand or grit that may get into an oyster or mussel shell. As layer upon layer of nacre coats the grit, a pearl is formed. This luminosity fostered the belief, long ago, that pearls were moonbeams that fell into the ocean and were eaten by oysters.

Healing Properties:
Pearls symbolize the moon, purity, spirituality, and virtue. The white pearl symbolizes the pure heart and mind. Pearls are soothing, reducing irritability. Because pearls are from the sea, they have water and lunar aspects and are said to balance the emotions. They contain the power of love. Ancient Greeks thought that wearing pearls would bring about marital happiness.

Peridot

Color & Physical Properties:
Peridot is the birthstone for August. They are a clear bright green and sometimes found in meteorites. Legend has it that one of Cleopatra's favorite emeralds was actually a peridot.

Healing Properties:
A good luck stone bringing protection, wealth, and health. Help us connect to our life's purpose or destiny. It was used by ancients to help heal the physical heart. Calms anger and dispels negative emotions and jealousy.

Rose Quartz

Color & Physical Properties:
This stone is a beautiful ballet pink color to a rosy red. It is a unique variety of quartz because the color is caused by impurities or iron and titanium.

Healing Properties:
Love, beauty, peacefulness, forgiveness, softness, and emotional balance are all healing qualities of rose quartz. Help us love and accept ourselves. It is often called the love stone because it can assist in emotional heart problems.

Ruby Quartz

Color & Physical Properties:
It is a fragile quartz variety. Ruby colored, sparkly inclusions in the stone are the source of the stone's name.

Healing Properties:
Stone of passion and vitality.
It is protective, and wards off aggression and violence. In crystal healing and traditional folklore, ruby quartz is used in healing the back, feet, hips, spine, and legs.

Serpentine

Color & Physical Properties:
It is light to dark green, with variations of color and inclusions that make it look like snake skin.

Healing Properties:
A good stone for meditation and protection for travelers. Relaxes one's overall nature. Heals the emotions. In ancient times it was worn as an amulet to protect one from snake bite.

continued from page 21

Snowflake Obsidian

Color & Physical Properties:
When used for jewelry, it has a polished black base with white snowflake-like inclusions. It is volcanic lava that has cooled quickly to form natural glass. The snowflakes are bits of hardened ash. It was one of the first stones used by native peoples to make weapons, such as arrowheads and knives.

Healing Properties:
Snowflake obsidian is a good stone to use in times of change. Promotes transformation. Believed to absorb and dissolve negativity, stress, fear. Helps transform negative energy into positive energy. Helps us recognize negative patterns in our lives.

Sodalite

Color & Physical Properties:
This stone is navy blue with white inclusions. Found in North America as well as in Brazil and France. Sodalite's high blue color is thought to be evidence of its spiritual significance.

Healing Properties:
Aids in healing, meditation, and acquisition of wisdom. Called the "writing stone" because it is believed to enhance communication, logic, ideas, and truth. It can strongly affect your attitude about yourself.

Tiger's Eye

Color & Physical Properties:
The stone is can be gold/yellow gold/brown, or yellow/brown with streaks. It is of the quartz family and sometimes called tiger iron. It has streaks of fibrous material that create landscape like patterns.

Healing Properties:
Gives inner strength and helps with decision making and creativity. Aids in achieving clarity and prospering in business. Promotes spiritual well being. A good stone to wear if you need more confidence to accomplish goals.

Topaz

Color & Physical Properties:
The birthstone for the month of November. The most common color is a radiant yellow; but it can be found in shades of blue, green, and brown. It is a very hard gemstone.

Healing Properties:
Assures true love and success in all endeavors. It is an excellent stone to promote relaxation since it is thought to calm the nervous system and lessen tension. Attracts love and prosperity.

Turquoise

Color & Physical Properties:
Turquoise is the birthstone for the month of December. It has a high copper content which gives the stone its color. The color can be turquoise, greenish blue, or sky blue shades. The name is related to the fact that the stone was brought to Europe by traders known as Turks. The book of Exodus refers to turquoise as one of the stones in the breastplate of the Hebrew high priest Aaron. Native Americans of the Southwestern United States believe turquoise connects earth and sky and it is one of their sacred stones. It is one of the four elemental gemstones of Pueblo Indians. (The others are coral, jet, and abalone shell.)

Healing Properties:
Used for mental relaxation, mental and spiritual clairity, stress reduction, and physical balance. Attracts prosperity and love. Relaxes the mind. Brings protection, courage, and luck. An ancient absorber of negativity. Turquoise was used to decorate the bridles of horses to protect them against broken bones from falls. It is a good general healer for all illnesses.

Bead Size Chart

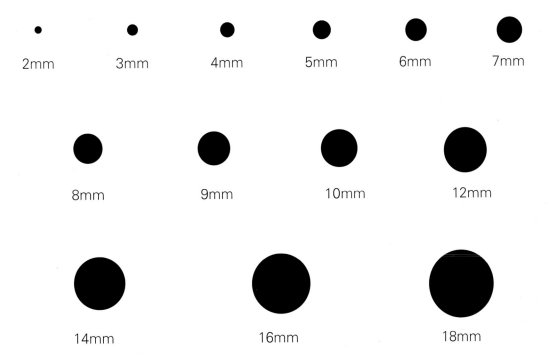

2mm   3mm   4mm   5mm   6mm   7mm

8mm   9mm   10mm   12mm

14mm   16mm   18mm

Number of Beads Needed for Necklace Lengths

Bead Size	16"	20"	24"	36"
3mm	130	170	200	300
4mm	100	127	150	225
6mm	67	85	100	150
8mm	50	63	75	113
10mm	40	50	60	90

If you are using a clasp, subtract a few beads to accommodate
the length of the clasp.

Healing Jewelry Projects

This section of the book contains instructions for nearly 50 beaded jewelry projects. There are necklaces of all kinds - long and short, casual and formal, refined and rustic. You'll find bracelets galore, strung on thread, on wire, on elastic cording. There are earrings to wear with coordinating necklaces and bracelets or on their own, and inventive brooches that will add zing and delight to bodice and lapel. There are also projects for beads meant for devotion and contemplation - a rosary, a mala, a prayer box necklace, and worry beads.

Each project includes a photograph, some information about the purported healing characteristics of the stone, a complete listing of supplies and tools, and step-by-step instructions. An array of how-to photos and figures show the details for making each piece. Patterns are provided when required.

Use them as guides or as inspiration for making your own one-of-a-kind creations.

LUSTROUS GLOW
citrine & carnelian chip bracelet

This bracelet combines the healing energies of carnelian and the spiritual boost of citrine. It feels substantial on the wrist and absorbs the warmth of your skin. The gemstone chips capture light and give off a lustrous glow.

Designed by Kaaren Poole

BEADING SUPPLIES

Drilled citrine chips

Drilled carnelian chips

Translucent topaz seed beads, size 6

Bronze seed beads, size 11

Translucent peach seed beads, size 11

4 crimp beads

Copper finish toggle clasp with a 12mm (or larger) ring

Beading wire

Gold beading thread, size D

TOOLS & OTHER SUPPLIES

Wire cutters

Beading needle, size 10

Beeswax *or* other thread conditioner

Small sharp scissors

Crimping tool

INSTRUCTIONS
Bracelet length: 7-1/2"

Make the Basic Bracelet:

1. Cut a piece of beading wire about 5" longer than you want the finished bracelet to be. (e.g., for a 7" bracelet, cut a 12" piece of wire.)

2. Thread two crimp beads on one end of the wire. Thread the wire through the ring on one piece of the toggle clasp. Push the end of the wire back through the two crimp beads. Adjust the crimp beads so they are snug against the clasp, leaving a 2" tail. With the crimping pliers, close the crimps securely. (Fig. A) Trim the tail to 1".

3. String the size 6 seed beads on the wire to the desired length of the bracelet. As you begin, slip the beads over the wire tail as well as the main wire.

4. Attach the other piece of the toggle clasp on the other end of the wire, using the two remaining crimp beads. Leave about 1/8" of space on the wire. (This 1/8" will provide the little spaces between the beads to allow for adding the gemstone beads.) Trim the tail to 1" and tuck it through the beads at the end of the wire.

Add the Carnelian Chips (First Pass):

1. Cut a 2 yd. piece of beading thread and pull it along the beeswax to condition it. Thread the beading needle. Tie a bronze seed bead to the end of the thread, leaving a 6" tail.

2. Thread the needle through the first size 6 seed beads next to the ring end of the clasp. Thread one bronze seed bead, one carnelian chip, then another bronze seed bead. Push the beads close to the bracelet. See Fig. B - Attaching a Chip String.

3. Skipping the seed bead closest to the needle, thread the needle back through the carnelian chip and the seed bead closest to the bracelet. Thread the needle through the next size 6 bead. Pull the thread snug, being sure that there is no extra space between the size 11 seed bead and the bracelet. (You have created a chip string.)

continued on next page

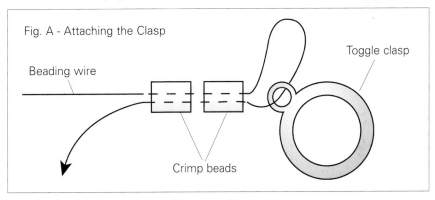

Fig. A - Attaching the Clasp

Beading wire

Toggle clasp

Crimp beads

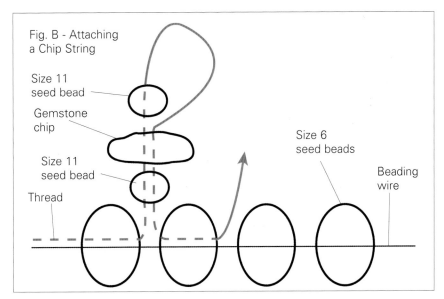

Fig. B - Attaching a Chip String

Size 11 seed bead

Gemstone chip

Size 11 seed bead

Thread

Size 6 seed beads

Beading wire

continued from page 27

4. Repeat to the end of the bracelet (the bead next to the bar end of the clasp). You will have a chip string between each size 6 seed bead in the bracelet. When you add the chip string past the last bead, thread the needle back through the same size 6 bead to turn.

Add the Citrine Chips (Second Pass):

1. Work the second pass in the opposite direction from the first (from the bar end to the ring end). The thread should be between the first two size 6 beads next to the bar end of the clasp. Thread the needle through two translucent peach size 11 seed beads, a citrine chip, then another translucent peach seed bead. Skipping the seed bead closet to the needle, thread the needle back through the citrine chip and the two translucent peach seed beads closest to the bracelet. Thread the needle through the next size 6 bead and pull the thread snug.

2. Repeat to the end of the bracelet (to the bead next to the ring end of the clasp). You now have two chip strings between each of the size 6 seed beads in the bracelet. Turn as before.

Add More Carnelian Chips (Third Pass):

1. Work the third pass back from the ring end to the bar end in the same manner as before. But for this pass, use three translucent peach size 11 seed beads, a carnelian chip, then another translucent peach seed bead for each chip string.

2. Continue to the bar end. You now have three chip strings between each size 6 seed bead.

Finish:

1. Knot the thread through the seed bead at the base of the last chip string. Thread the needle and thread back through several of the size 6 seed beads. Trim the end of the thread.

2. Thread the beginning thread tail on the needle and thread it through several of the size 6 seed beads. Trim the end of the thread. ❏

TRINITY
shell bracelet

BEADING SUPPLIES

18 abalone shell beads, 8x18mm
54 faceted labradorite rondelles, 4mm to 5mm
6 silver crimp beads
1 silver 3-into-1 connector with lobster clasp
2 silver 3-hole spacer tubes, 14mm
2 silver jump rings
Beading wire, .015

TOOLS & OTHER SUPPLIES

Wire cutters
Crimping tool

INSTRUCTIONS
Bracelet length: 8"

1. Attach one side of the lobster clasp to the 3-into-1 connector with a jump ring.

2. Cut three 12" lengths of bead stringing wire. Thread a crimp bead on one end of each wire. Wrap each wire end around a hole in the 3-into-1 connector, then back through the crimp bead leaving a 1" tail. Crimp beads.

3. On the outer two rows, thread an abalone shell bead, three labradorite rondelles, an abalone shell bead, and three labradorite rondelles, stringing the beads over the wire tails.

4. Add a 3-hole spacer tube to each outer row.

5. On the center row, thread three labradorite rondelles, an abalone shell bead, three labradorite rondelles, and an abalone shell bead. Thread the wire through the center hole of the 3-hole spacer tube.

6. Repeat steps 3, 4, and 5 two more times, ending with 3-into-1 connector instead of a spacer tube.

7. Thread a crimp bead on each wire end. Wrap each wire end around a hole in the 3-into-1 connector, then back through the crimp bead and several beads. Pull wires taut. Crimp beads.

8. Attach the other side of the lobster clasp to the 3-into-1 connector with a jump ring. ❏

TRINITY
shell bracelet

This three-strand bracelet combines the rainbow colors of abalone shell beads, labradorite rondelles, and silver. Labradorite is believed to bring forth personal strength and help one relate to others. Wearing it in a bracelet can help you reach out and connect with others.

Designed by Patty Cox

PEACEFUL SEAS
braided pearl bracelet

This bracelet combines glowing mother-of-pearl beads in two colors and lustrous natural pearls to bring the peaceful healing energy of the sea to your wrist. The instructions for coral earrings follow on page 32.

Designed by Patty Cox

BEADING SUPPLIES

Coral rainbow seed beads

80 (approx.) pink shell mother of pearl beads, 4mm

60 (approx.) natural mother of pearl beads, 5mm

50 (approx.) ivory blush freshwater potato pearls, 6mm

1 silver two-strand box clasp, 10mm

4 silver crimp beads

Beading wire, .014, flexible type

Optional: 4 silver bead tips

TOOLS & OTHER SUPPLIES

Wire cutters

Crimping tool

Masking tape

Photo sequence below:

Braiding the strands: Hold the seed bead strand and pearl strand together as one while braiding.

INSTRUCTIONS
Bracelet length - 9"

Attach Wires to the Clasp:

1. Cut four 16" strands of flexible beading wire.
2. Thread a silver crimp bead on two wires. Thread the two wires through one hole on one side of the box clasp. Fold the wires over the box clasp hole, then back through the crimp bead. Slide the crimp bead close to the box clasp. Crimp the bead.
3. Repeat step 2 to secure the remaining two wires in the second hole of the box clasp.

Add the Beads:

Thread 11-1/2" of beads on each wire to make four strands:

    Strand #1 - Coral seed beads

    Strand #2 - 6mm pearls

    Strand #3 - Alternating 5mm mother of pearl beads and coral seed beads

    Strand #4 - 4mm pink mother of pearl beads.

As you begin each strand, thread the beads over the short wire end near the clasp. When you get to the end of a strand, wrap a piece of masking tape around it to secure beads in position.

Braid:

See Photos 1 through 5.

Hold the seed bead and pearls together as one strand while braiding. Braid the strands to their ends, following the sequence in the photos.

Finish:

1. To attach the strands to the other side of the box clasp, remove the masking tape from two strands and hold the wire ends of those strands together. Thread a crimp bead over the wires. Thread the two wires through one hole in the box clasp. Fold the wires over box clasp hole, then back through crimp bead. Slide the crimp bead close to the box clasp. Crimp the bead.
2. Repeat the process to attach the remaining two strands in the second hole of the box clasp.
3. Thread the short wire ends back through several beads on each strand. Cut wire ends.
4. *Option:* Cover crimp beads with silver bead tips. ❏

Photo 1	*Photo 2*	*Photo 3*	*Photo 4*	*Photo 5*

DELICATE BRANCHES
coral & pearl earrings

Seed beads are strung on thread to resemble delicate branches of sea coral and are accented with natural pearls. Pearls are believed to balance emotions and reduce irritability.

Designed by Patty Cox

BEADING SUPPLIES

2 pkgs. coral rainbow seed beads (8 grams total)
1 pkg. crystal matte seed beads (4 grams total)
2 ivory blush fresh water potato pearls, 6mm
2 silver ear wires
Beading thread

TOOLS & OTHER SUPPLIES

Beading needle
Scissors

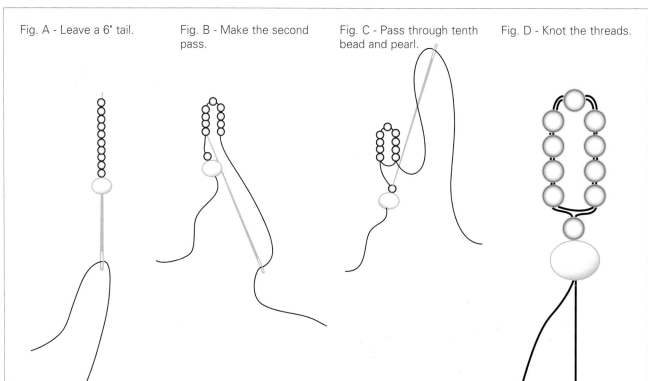

Fig. A - Leave a 6" tail.

Fig. B - Make the second pass.

Fig. C - Pass through tenth bead and pearl.

Fig. D - Knot the threads.

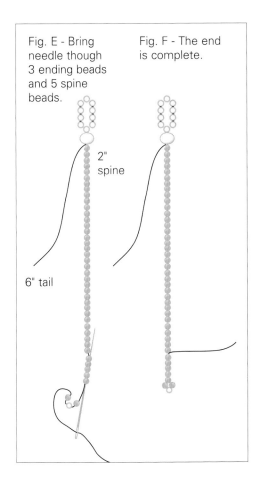

Fig. E - Bring needle though 3 ending beads and 5 spine beads.

Fig. F - The end is complete.

2" spine

6" tail

INSTRUCTIONS

These instructions are for making one earring. Repeat to make the second earring.

Make the Hanging Loop:

1. Thread a beading needle with 42" of beading thread.
2. Thread 10 crystal beads and one 6mm pearl on the needle (Fig. A). Slide beads near the thread end, leaving a 6" tail.
3. Pass the needle and thread back through nine beads, forming a loop (Fig. B).
4. Thread the needle through the tenth bead and the pearl, securing the loop (Fig. C). Knot the thread tails under the pearl (Fig. D).

Make the Central Spine:

1. Add 2" of coral beads (about 40) on the needle and thread. Slide the beads under the pearl. Add three ending beads - coral, crystal, coral (Fig. E). Bring needle around the ending beads and back into the spine.
2. Thread the needle through the lower five spine beads. Bring out the needle (Fig. F). Pull the thread so the beads are tight and close together.

Make the Branches on the Central Spine:

1. Add four coral beads and three ending beads - coral, crystal, coral (Fig. G).

Continued on next page

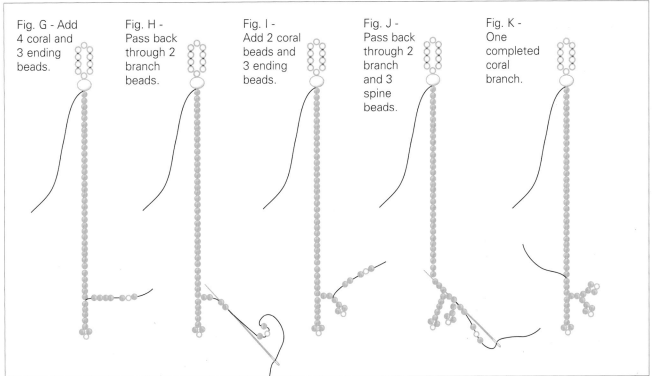

Fig. G - Add 4 coral and 3 ending beads.

Fig. H - Pass back through 2 branch beads.

Fig. I - Add 2 coral beads and 3 ending beads.

Fig. J - Pass back through 2 branch and 3 spine beads.

Fig. K - One completed coral branch.

Continued from page 33

2. Bring the needle around ending the beads and back into the branch. Thread the needle through two branch beads. Tighten the thread tension. Bring out the needle (Fig. H).

3. Add two coral beads and three ending beads (Fig. I). Bring the needle around the ending beads and back into the branch. Thread the needle through three spine beads and tighten the thread tension. Bring the needle out (Fig. J). You have completed one coral branch (Fig. K). Each coral branch is made the same way, following the process shown in Figs. G through K - simply count up three beads on the spine and add a new branch. Keep the thread tension tight throughout beading.

Add Short Spines with Branches:

1. When the last branch has been made on the central spine, bring the needle through the remaining spine beads and out at the top of the spine under the pearl. Tie the beading thread, leaving a 6" tail (Fig. L).

2. Start a new (second) spine with the same beading thread. Make the spine 1-1/2" long (about 30 beads).

3. Make branches on this second spine, following the process in Figs. G through K.

4. Bring the needle through the remaining spine beads, then out at the top of the spine under the pearl. Tie the beading thread, leaving a 6" tail.

5. Make a third (last) 1-1/2" spine the same way as the second. Bring the needle up through spine and out under pearl at the top of the spine. Knot the threads (Fig. M).

6. Run the thread ends back through three or more beads. Cut the thread ends. ❑

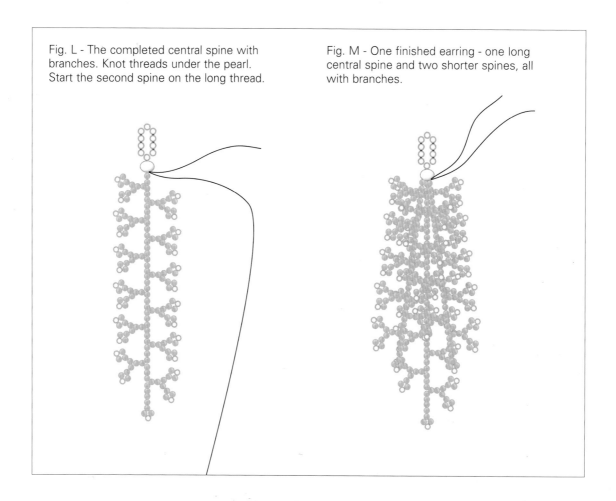

Fig. L - The completed central spine with branches. Knot threads under the pearl. Start the second spine on the long thread.

Fig. M - One finished earring - one long central spine and two shorter spines, all with branches.

SPARKLE & GLOW
citrine bracelet

Citrine gets its name from its yellow color - *citron* is the French word for
lemon. Citrine is believed to promote a bright and happy disposition.
Wear this when you wish to portray a positive attitude.

Designed by Patty Cox

Instructions begin on page 36.

SPARKLE & GLOW
citrine bracelet

BEADING SUPPLIES

90 (approx.) citrine faceted rondelles, 5mm

Transparent gold matte seed beads

15 (approx.) 24-kt. gold-plated
beads, 2.4mm

1 gold toggle clasp

2 yds. white beading thread

TOOLS & OTHER SUPPLIES

Beading needle

Scissors

Also pictured on page 35

INSTRUCTIONS
Bracelet length: 8"

Make the Central Strand:

1. Thread a beading needle with 2 yds. beading thread. Attach and knot one end of the thread to one part of the toggle clasp, leaving a 3" tail.
2. Thread on a seed bead, a gold bead, a seed bead, and three citrine rondelles. Repeat this beading sequence to make a strand 7-1/4" long. (Fig. A) *Option:* Make the strand the length you desire.
3. Tie the other half of the toggle clasp on the end of the beaded strand.

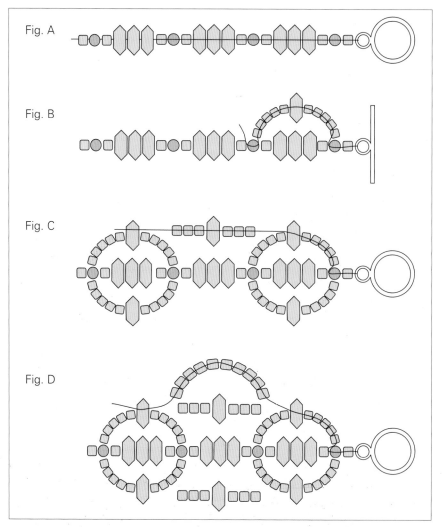

Fig. A

Fig. B

Fig. C

Fig. D

Add the Other Beads:

1. Starting at the end of the strand, thread the needle back through a seed bead and a gold bead. Thread five seed beads, a citrine rondelle, and five seed beads and run the needle and thread through the gold bead. (Fig. B) Repeat the process to add beaded scallops on both sides of the central strand. (Photo 1, Photo 2)

2. Run the needle and thread back through the first gold bead and seed bead, then around the toggle clasp. Pass the thread back through the seed bead and gold bead, the first five seed beads, and the citrine rondelle on the scallop. Add three seed beads, a citrine rondelle, and three more seed beads and thread the needle through the next citrine rondelle. (Fig. C) Repeat the process, adding beads between the scallops on both sides of the bracelet. (Photo 3, Photo 4)

3. Pass the needle back through beginning beads and around the toggle clasp. Thread the needle through the beads of the first scallop and citrine rondelle. Thread 10 seed beads on the needle and pass through the next citrine rondelle to make a second row of scallops. (Fig. D) Repeat the process to continue adding more scallops on both sides of the bracelet. (Photo 5, Photo 6)

Finish:

Pass the needle back through the beads next to the toggle clasp, then around the clasp. Knot the thread around the clasp. Run the thread back through several beads. Cut the thread. Thread the 3" tail on the needle. Run the thread through several beads. Cut the thread. ❑

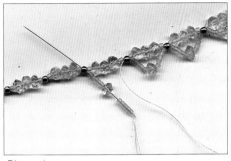

Photo 1

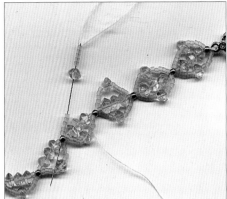

Photo 2

Photo 3

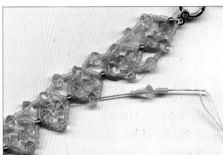

Photo 4

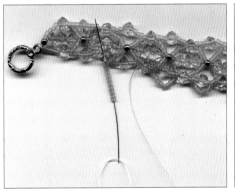

Photo 5

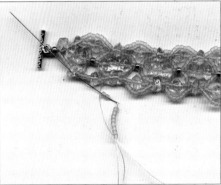

Photo 6

CELTIC CARNELIAN
brooch

This brooch, which showcases a large carnelian cabochon, is loosely based on a simple Celtic knot. The knot has no beginning or end and so is a symbol of eternity. Carnelian reminds us to be "in the moment" - it is a stone of protection, particularly from anger and fear. Gazing into the stone's warm red color can bring a sense of calm and an understanding and acceptance of the great cycle of life.

The brooch also includes pearls, which are beautiful and soothing, reflecting the pearl's creation, in which an oyster transforms an irritant into an object of lustrous beauty.

Designed by Kaaren Poole

BEADING SUPPLIES

1 carnelian cabochon, 30x40mm

5 carnelian flat oval beads,
8x10mm

3 button-shaped pearls, 8mm

8 bicone jet crystal beads, 4mm

Seed beads, size 11

Transparent crystal AB

Lined peach AB

Translucent gold topaz

Translucent dusty rose brown

Transparent light peach

Translucent coffee

Gold beading thread, size D

Stiff beading foundation,
4" x 4-1/2"

TOOLS & OTHER SUPPLIES

Pin back with 1" circular pad

Sharp needle, size 5 (small sharp-
pointed sewing needle with a
small eye)

Beeswax *or* thread conditioner

Pencil

Clear cement

Small sharp scissors

Plastic knife

Synthetic suede fabric, 4" x 4-1/2"
(for backing)

Waterbase non-toxic super glue

INSTRUCTIONS

Start:

1. Place the piece of beading foundation over the pattern. Trace the pattern on the beading foundation with a pencil.
2. Using clear cement, glue the cabochon in place. **Do not** get any glue beyond the cabochon. Let dry overnight.
3. Using a backstitch, stitch a ring of beads around the central cabochon, alternating between translucent coffee and transparent light peach. See Fig. A. Run a thread back through all the beads in the ring to align them.

Bead the Bands:

See Fig. A.

1. Bead one row in one question mark-shaped section with lined Peach AB seed beads. Run a thread through each bead in the row to align it.
2. Bead a second row next to the first and run a thread through each bead to align it.
3. Repeat the previous steps to bead the question mark-shaped section counterclockwise from the previous one, but use transparent light peach seed beads. Begin your rows at the outside edge of the previous question mark-shaped band.
4. Repeat the process to complete the remaining question mark sections.

Sew the Carnelian Beads & Pearls:

1. Sew each carnelian bead in place, looping thread through the bead three times to secure it. Knot the thread after sewing each bead.
2. Sew each pearl in place. Bring the thread up through the beading foundation at the center of the space for the pearl. Bring the thread through the

continued on next page

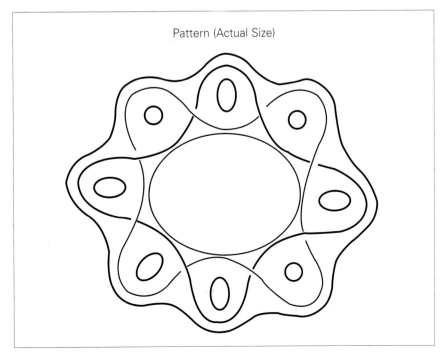

Pattern (Actual Size)

continued from page 39

pearl from bottom to top, then through a transparent crystal AB seed bead. Bring the thread back down through the pearl from top to bottom, then down through the beading foundation. Pull the thread snug and knot it.

Add the Rest of the Beads:

1. Fill the sections of the Celtic knot with translucent gold topaz and transparent crystal AB seed beads, back-stitching each bead in place and placing the colors according to the Beading Diagram (Fig. A). Do not attempt to line up the beads; sewing them in random directions gives a glittery look.
2. Back-stitch a row of translucent coffee beads around the outside edge of the design. Run a thread back through the row to align it.
3. Fill the areas between the outer edge and the knot sections by back-stitching translucent dusty rose brown seed beads in random directions.
4. Sew the jet crystals in place, looping through the beads two or three times to secure them. Knot the thread after each bead.

Finish:

1. With small sharp scissors, carefully cut away the excess beading foundation. Be careful not to cut any of the threads.
2. Use the plastic knife to generously apply non-toxic super glue to the back of the piece. Be sure to cover all of the threads, especially around the edge. Lay the beaded piece on the synthetic suede. Press firmly over the entire piece for good contact. Let dry overnight.
3. Carefully trim away the excess synthetic suede.
4. Again using non-toxic super glue, glue the pin back in place. Let dry thoroughly. ❏

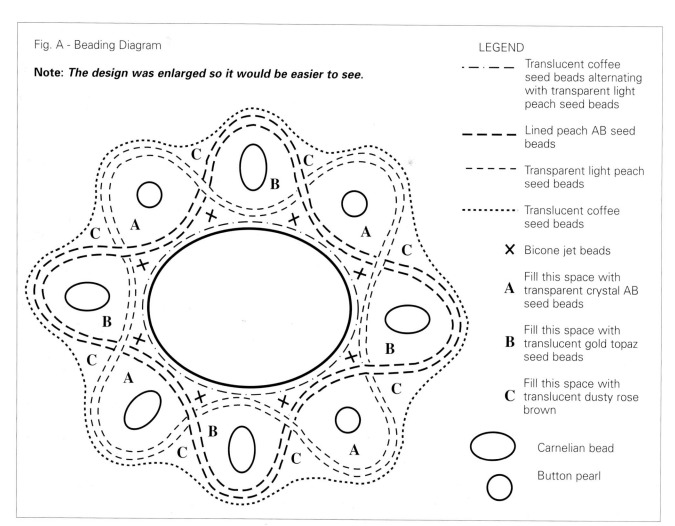

Fig. A - Beading Diagram

Note: *The design was enlarged so it would be easier to see.*

MALACHITE ON A WIRE
ear loops

Malachite is believed to improve mental strength and stabilize the psyche.
Here, malachite beads are strung on thin wire that's wrapped around
a more substantial wire framing three beaded dangles.

Designed by Kathi Bailey

BEADING SUPPLIES

26 malachite beads, 6mm

Blue/green/gold mixed seed beads, size 11/0

Blue/green/gold mixed seed beads, size 6/0

Gold wire, 22mm

Gold wire, 18mm

2 gold jump rings, 10mm

2 earring wires

4 eye pins, 1"

2 head pins, 1-1/2"

4 gold metal bead drops with cap

TOOLS & OTHER SUPPLIES

Needlenose pliers

Wire cutters

Beading glue

Roundnose pliers

INSTRUCTIONS

1. Cut two 5" lengths of 18mm wire. Create a loop at each end of each piece, using roundnose pliers.

2. Cut two 6" lengths of 22mm wire. Place ten malachite beads on each wire, spacing the beads evenly along the lengths. Twist the one beaded wire around one of the 18mm wire pieces. Wrap the ends of the beaded wire around the 18mm wire.

3. Bead each eye pin with one malachite bead, two seed beads, one clear bead, and one seed bead. Make a loop in the end of each eye pin, using roundnose pliers.

4. Insert a bead drop into each of four malachite beads and glue to secure. Let dry. Attach a malachite bead on a bead drop on the end of each eye pin, using the photo as a guide.

5. Bead each head pin with one malachite bead, five 6/0 seed beads, two clear seed beads, and four seed beads. Trim the ends of the head pins to 3/8". Make a loop in the end of each head pin, using roundnose pliers.

6. Curve one 5" piece of 18mm wire into a semi-circle. Loop one end on an opened gold ring. Follow with one beaded eye pin, one beaded head pin, one beaded eye pin, and the loop on the other end of the wire. Close the ring.

7. Attach to earring wire.

8. Repeat steps 6 and 7 to complete the other earring. ❏

CIRCLE OF LIFE
honeybee brooch

BEADING SUPPLIES

1 diamond-shaped blue-gray pearl, 10x18mm

2 rice-shaped freshwater pearls, 5x7mm

4 button-shaped freshwater pearls, 4mm

9 citrine chips

9 moonstone chips

9 bicone crystals, 4mm (assorted pale blues and greens)

2 bicone jet crystals, 6mm

Iris bronze bugle beads

Round seed beads, size 11:

    Pearly off-white

    Metallic gold

    Iris dark blue

    Transparent bronze

    Ceylon aqua (a translucent rainbow finish)

    Transparent rainbow aqua (a transparent bead with a rainbow reflective finish)

    Transparent rainbow crystal

    Transparent rainbow lime green

    Transparent rainbow champagne

    Ceylon light yellow

    Transparent yellow

White beading thread, size D

Stiff beading foundation, 3-1/2" x 4-1/2"

TOOLS & OTHER SUPPLIES

Pin back with 1" circular pad

Size 5 sharp sewing needle with a small eye

Beeswax *or* other thread conditioner

Pencil

Waterbase non-toxic super glue

Small sharp scissors

Plastic knife

Synthetic suede fabric, 3-1/2" x 4-1/2" (for backing)

INSTRUCTIONS

(See Fig. A - Beading Diagram on page 44.)

Bead the Outlines:

1. Place the piece of beading foundation over the pattern. Trace the pattern on the beading foundation with a pencil.
2. Backstitch the outer row of metallic gold beads, including one iris dark blue bead at the end of each feeler. Work in two sections - above the wings and below them. Run a thread back through each bead in the rows to align them.
3. Backstitch the outlines of the wings with off-white pearly beads. Run the thread back through the lines of beads to align them.
4. Backstitch the lines of transparent rainbow champagne seed beads.
5. Backstitch the shorter lines of pearly finish beads within the wings.

Bead the Bee's Upper Body:

1. Sew the central diamond-shaped pearl in place, looping the thread through the pearl three or four times to secure it. Knot the thread.
2. Work the upper part of the body. Backstitch two rows of transparent yellow beads along the upper edges of the diamond-shaped pearl.
3. Sew the two jet bicone beads in place for the eyes.
4. Sew each leg, backstitching an iris bronze bugle bead for the upper leg, then three transparent bronze seed beads for the feet.

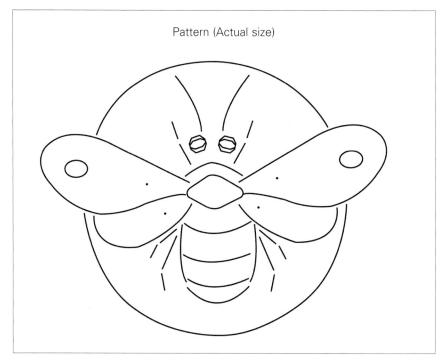

Pattern (Actual size)

Kaaren designed this piece around one of her favorite images, the honeybee, a powerful symbol of the life force. Most of the design is worked in round seed beads, but the center of the design - the honeybee's thorax - is a diamond-shaped pearl, and smaller pearls grace the wings. Pearls are beautiful and soothing, reflecting their creation, in which an oyster covers an irritant in its shell with layer upon layer of luster. Chips of citrine (for happiness) and moonstone (to soothe stress and anxiety) appear in the fringe.

Designed by Kaaren Poole

5. Backstitch lines of iris dark blue seed beads for the feelers.
6. Fill the head with the same dark blue beads.

Bead the Bee's Lower Body:
1. Backstitch a row of iris dark blue seed beads along the lower edge of the diamond-shaped pearl.
2. Backstitch three rows of yellow beads below the dark blue ones. Use transparent yellow for the upper row. For the middle row, stitch two Ceylon light yellow beads at each end and transparent yellow in the center. For the lower row, use Ceylon light yellow.
3. Backstitch the outline of the lower body (below the yellow stripe), using iris dark blue at the edges of the dark stripes and Ceylon light yellow at the edges of the yellow stripe.
4. Fill the upper dark stripe with iris bronze bugle beads.
5. Fill the yellow stripe with Ceylon light yellow seed beads.
6. Fill the lowest dark stripe with iris dark blue seed beads.

continued on next page

continued from page 43

7. Backstitch the legs with an iris bronze bugle bead for the upper leg and transparent bronze seed beads for the feet. Use four seed beads on the lower legs and two on the others.

Finish the Wings:

1. Sew the rice-shaped pearls in place on the wings, looping the thread through the pearls two or three times to secure them. Knot the thread after each pearl.
2. To attach the button pearls, bring the thread up through the foundation and through the pearl, flat side first. Bring the thread through a transparent rainbow crystal bead then back down through the pearl and the backing. Knot the thread after sewing each pearl.
3. Fill the remaining areas of the wings with transparent rainbow crystal seed beads. Backstitch each one in place. Don't try to line them up - sewing them in random directions gives a glittery look.

Finish the Background:

1. To work the background, backstitch rows of beads parallel to the outer gold row. Begin next to the gold with Ceylon aqua. The next row inward in transparent rainbow aqua. As you work, run a thread back through each row to align it.
2. Continue the background with transparent rainbow lime green. Work even rows as far as you can, then fill the remaining areas randomly.

Work the Fringe:

1. To begin, weave the end of the thread through the various threads on the back of the piece to secure it.
2. Bring the thread through the center bead of the lower gold trim line. For the first (center) string of fringe, thread these beads on the thread: five metallic gold seed beads, one citrine chip, three transparent crystal rainbow beads, one moonstone chip, one transparent rainbow crystal bead, one 4mm bicone crystal, and one transparent rainbow crystal seed bead.

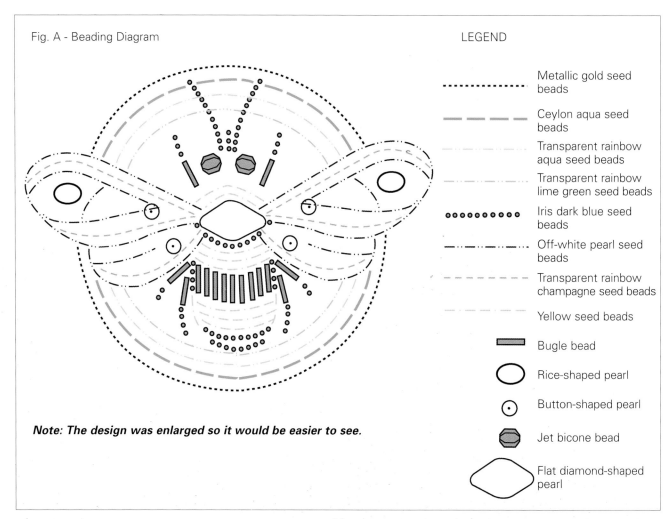

Fig. A - Beading Diagram

LEGEND

- · · · · · · · · Metallic gold seed beads
- — — — Ceylon aqua seed beads
- — · — · — Transparent rainbow aqua seed beads
- — · · — · · — Transparent rainbow lime green seed beads
- ••••••••• Iris dark blue seed beads
- — — — Off-white pearl seed beads
- — — — Transparent rainbow champagne seed beads
- — — — Yellow seed beads
- ▬ Bugle bead
- ◯ Rice-shaped pearl
- ⊙ Button-shaped pearl
- ⬡ Jet bicone bead
- ◇ Flat diamond-shaped pearl

Note: The design was enlarged so it would be easier to see.

3. Bring the needle back through the bicone crystal (skip the last seed bead), transparent rainbow seed bead, moonstone chip, three transparent rainbow seed beads, citrine chip, and five metallic gold seed beads and pull the thread snug. Now you are back at the gold trim row.
4. Working to the left, bring the thread through two metallic gold beads on the trim row, then work the next string of fringe. The only difference in this string from the first one is that this one begins with four gold metallic beads instead of five.
5. Continuing to the left, work the remaining three strings according to Fig. B - Fringe Diagram.
6. Thread back through the gold beads on the trim row, bringing the needle out after two gold metallic beads to the right of the central fringe string. Work the four strings on the right side of the fringe. See Fig. B.

Finish:
1. With small sharp scissors, carefully trim the excess beading foundation. Be careful not to cut any of the threads, and be **extremely** careful while cutting near the fringe.
2. Use the plastic knife to generously apply waterbase non-toxic super glue to the back of the piece. Be sure to cover all of the threads, especially around the edge, but don't get any glue on the fringe. Lay the beaded piece on the synthetic suede. Press firmly over the entire piece for good contact. Let dry overnight.
3. Carefully trim away the excess synthetic suede.
4. Again using non-toxic super glue, glue the pin back in place. Let dry thoroughly. ❑

Fig. B - Fringe Diagram

LEGEND

◯ Gold metallic seed bead (in outline)

◯ Gold metallic seed bead (in fringe)

▱ Citrine chip

▱ Moonstone chip

◯ Transparent rainbow crystal seed bead

⬡ Bicone crystal bead

SERPENTINE SECURITY
two-disc choker

Serpentine enhances one's sense of security and promotes relaxation and healing of all disorders of the body and mind. Here, two serpentine discs are knotted on waxed cotton cord and combined with green cat's eye and matte glass beads.

Designed by Patty Cox

BEADING SUPPLIES

2 serpentine discs, 28mm

2 emerald matte glass flattened round beads, 14mm

4 emerald matte glass oval beads, 8x12mm

2 emerald matte glass round beads, 9mm

7 pastel green cat's eye round glass beads, 8mm

2 pastel green cat's eye round glass beads, 6mm

4 yds. pastel green waxed cotton cord, 2mm

1 silver toggle clasp

2 silver large-hole spacer beads *or* 2 coil spacers

2 wraparound leather end crimps (cut off the eyes)

TOOLS & OTHER SUPPLIES

Scissors

Corsage pin

Beading glue

INSTRUCTIONS

Necklace length: 16"

1. Fold a 4 yd. length cotton cord in half. Thread the cord through the one serpentine disc, making a lark's head knot as shown in Photo 1 through 4.
2. Thread an 8mm cat's eye bead on both cord ends, placing the bead next to the lark's head knot. Tie an overhand knot in both cords above the bead. Separate the cords.

continued on page 48

Making a Lark's Head Knot

Photo 1. Fold cord in half to form a loop. Thread through center hole.

Photo 2. Thread cord ends through the cord loop.

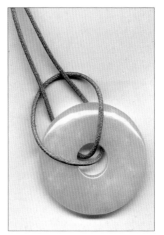

Photo 3. Pull cord ends.

Photo 4. A completed lark's head knot.

continued from page 46

3. Loop one cord through the center of the second serpentine disc. Thread the cord end through the loop. Pull the loop tightly around the disc. Make five knotted loops on the disc on each side of the disc (Photo 5).

4. Add a 6mm pastel cat's eye bead to each cord. Tie a knot in cord close to the bead. Use a corsage pin to position the knot next to the bead (Photo 6).

5. Continue threading beads on each cord to complete both sides of the necklace, knotting the cord after each bead, in this sequence: 14mm emerald matte flattened round, 8mm cat's eye, 8x12mm emerald matte oval, 8mm cat's eye, 8x12mm emerald matte oval, 8mm cat's eye, 9mm emerald matte round.

6. Thread a large hole spacer, then half of the toggle clasp on one side of the cord. Tie the toggle clasp half on the cord 3-1/4" from the last bead. Thread the cord tail back through the spacer bead (Photo 7). Slide the spacer bead over the knot.

7. With the cord tail, tie overhand knots or half hitches over the 3-1/4" of the necklace cord. The continuous knots will spiral around the cord (Photo 8). Dot the last knot with glue. Wrap a leather end crimp around the last knot. Cut cord end close to crimp.

8. Repeat steps 6 and 7 to attach the other side of the toggle clasp and finish the other side of the necklace. ❏

Photo 6. Use a corsage pin to position the knot next to the bead.

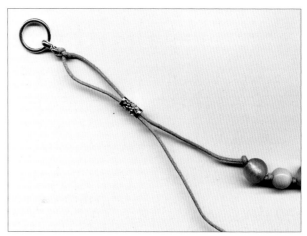

Photo 7. Tie the toggle clasp on the cord 3-1/4" from the last bead. Thread the cord tail back through the spacer bead.

Photo 5. Loop cord through center hole. Thread cord end through loop. Pull tight.

Photo 8. Tie continuous half hitch knots over the cord. The knots will spiral around the cord.

LEAVES OF CLAY
earrings

Amazonite creates feelings of power and inspires confidence. It is believed to reduce self-damaging and self-destructive behavior and eliminate irritation and aggravation. In these earrings, amazonite beads dangle from leaves formed from polymer clay.

Designed by Kathi Bailey

BEADING SUPPLIES

6 amazonite beads, 8mm

Blue/white/gold mixed seed beads, size 11/0

4 crimp beads

2 earring backs

Lightweight wire

TOOLS & OTHER SUPPLIES

Polymer clay, 1/4 oz. *each* - Mint, gold, white

Needlenose pliers

Wire cutters

Polymer clay knife

Large needle

White glue

Crimping tool

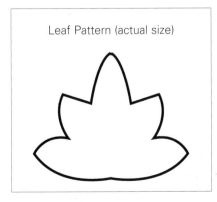

Leaf Pattern (actual size)

INSTRUCTIONS
Make the Clay Leaves:

1. Knead and roll each block of clay into cylinders. Twist together and knead again lightly.
2. Roll into two balls of approximately equal size and flatten to approximately 1/4" thickness.
3. Trace the leaf pattern on each piece of clay. Cut out with the knife.
4. Insert the needle in the bottom of each leaf to make a hole for attaching the beaded wire.
5. Bake leaves according to the clay manufacturer's instructions. Allow to cool.

Assemble:

1. Cut two 3" strands of wire. Fold each wire double. Add a crimp bead at the bottom (looped) end of each.
2. Twist each double wire and add beads, starting from the end with the crimp bead: one seed bead, 1 amazonite, one seed bead, one amazonite, one seed bead, one amazonite, and five seed beads.
3. Insert the end of the wire through the hole in one leaf. Add a crimp bead and crimp on the back side of the leaf.
4. Repeat steps 2 and 3 to make the other earring.
5. Glue earring backs to backs of leaves. ❏

MALACHITE BUTTERFLY
necklace or brooch

A powerful healing stone - malachite - and a symbol of transformation - the butterfly - join forces in this beautiful brooch. A removable bead rope allows the piece to double as a necklace. There are also pearls, which are beautiful and soothing, as well as green aventurine and chryophase. Aventurine lessens negativity and boosts the ability to see possibilities. Chryophase strengthens personal courage.

Designed by Kaaren Poole

the brooch

BEADING SUPPLIES
1 malachite cabochon, 18x25mm
2 flat diamond-shaped gray-blue pearls, 11x18mm
4 green aventurine cabochons, 6x8mm
2 round chryophase beads, 6mm
6 malachite rondelle beads, 6mm
2 button-shaped freshwater pearls, 4mm
2 button-shaped freshwater pearls, 7mm
2 bicone sapphire blue crystals, 4mm
20" (approx.) malachite beads, 2mm *or* round teal seed beads, size 11
Rainbow-finish mint green round seed beads, size 11
Cylinder seed beads, size 11:
    Hex-cut crystal AB
    Transparent light tan AB
    Lined round aqua
    Lined light blue
    Round transparent light blue
    Translucent round lime
    Translucent round sky blue
    Lined blue lustre
    Frost mint green

2 split rings, 8mm
2 head pins, 2-1/2" .028" diameter (or thin enough to go through the bead holes)
Dark green beading thread, size D
White beading thread, size D
Gold beading thread, size D
Stiff beading foundation, 4" x 5" piece

TOOLS & OTHER SUPPLIES
Pin back
Size 5 sharp sewing needle (sharp needle with a small eye)
Beeswax *or* other thread conditioner
Pencil
Clear cement
Small sharp scissors
Plastic knife
Synthetic suede fabric, 4" x 5" (for backing)
Waterbase non-toxic super glue

TIP: Malachite beads can be pricey and difficult to find for sale individually. If you like, use all chips for the rope and substitute chips for the rondelle malachite beads on the butterfly wings. The stone has the same healing properties whatever the shape!

INSTRUCTIONS
Start:
1. Place the piece of beading foundation over the pattern. Trace the pattern on the beading foundation with a pencil.
2. Use clear cement to glue the central cabochon in place. **Do not** get any glue beyond the cabochon. Let dry overnight.

Outline:
See Fig. A - Beading Diagram.
Begin the beading by outlining the central cabochon and the wings, using dark green thread. The project photo shows 2mm malachite beads, but round teal size 11 seed beads may be substituted. The holes in the malachite beads are very tiny. If you use them, you must string them on a length of thread (no needle), then apply the lines by couching (stitching the thread between the beads to the background - see Fig. B). If you use seed beads, backstitch the lines (see Fig. C), then run a thread back through the lines to align them.

Begin Filling the Wings:
Work the rest of the piece with white thread. See Fig. A - Beading Diagram and Fig. C - Backstitching.

continued on page 52

continued from page 50

1. Sew the diamond-shaped pearls in place, looping the thread through each pearl three or four times to secure it. Knot the thread after each pearl.

2. Sew the malachite rondelles and remaining pearls in place. Bring the thread up through the foundation at the point where the center of the bead will be. Run the thread up through the bead or pearl, then through a Crystal AB seed bead. Run the thread back down through the bead or pearl, then back through the foundation at the same place you started. Knot the thread after each bead or pearl. (The small cabochons come later.)

3. Backstitch the blue veins in the wings with lined blue luster beads. Run the thread back through all the beads in each line to align them.

Work the Upper Wings:

1. Backstitch the rings around each of the malachite rondelle beads and the connecting lines with ceylon mint green seed beads.

2. Fill the area with lined round aqua beads. Place them in lines following the outer edge of the area where possible, and fill in randomly otherwise.

3. Fill the small areas at the top of the wing with frost mint green beads. Sew the beads in lines parallel to the edge of the wing where possible.

4. Backstitch one row of round transparent light blue seed beads around the diamond-shaped pearls, then a row of hex-cut crystal AB seed beads around the first row. Fill the remaining area with crystal AB seed beads.

Work the Lower Wings:

1. Backstitch a ring of translucent round lime seed beads around the larger pearls.

2. Stitch a ring of translucent round sky blue seed beads around the lime ring.

3. Add a ring of transparent light tan AB seed beads around the sky blue ring.

4. Fill the remaining area with translucent round sky blue beads.

5. Fill the small areas at the bottom of

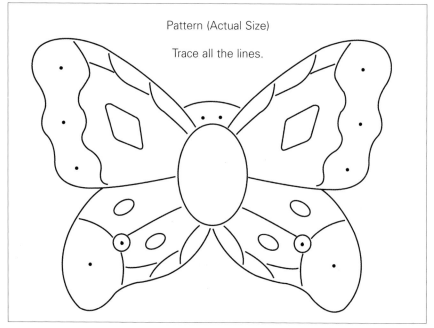

Pattern (Actual Size)

Trace all the lines.

the wings with frost mint green seed beads. the beads in rows parallel to the blue veins where possible.

6. Glue the small green aventurine cabochons in place with clear cement. Let dry thoroughly.

7. Backstitch a ring of transparent light tan AB seed beads around the upper cabochon. Fill the remaining area with the same beads. Be careful not to crowd the small cabochons - the pressure could pop them off the backing!

8. Backstitch a ring of lined light blue seed beads around the lower cabochon. Fill the outer portion of the area (away from the body) with the same color. Fill the inner portion with transparent light tan AB beads.

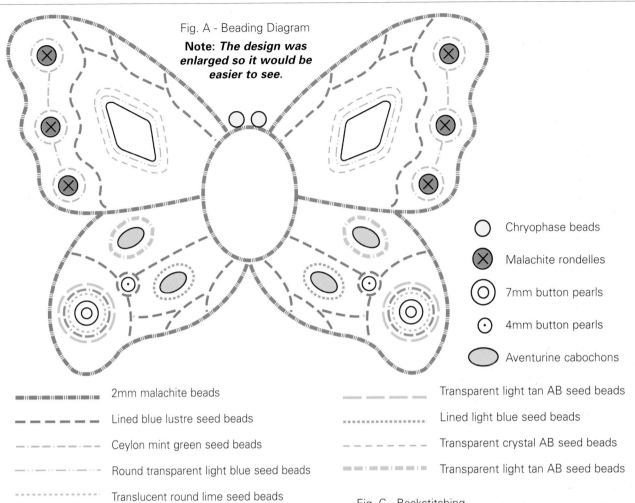

Fig. A - Beading Diagram

Note: *The design was enlarged so it would be easier to see.*

○ Chryophase beads

⊗ Malachite rondelles

◎ 7mm button pearls

⊙ 4mm button pearls

⬭ Aventurine cabochons

▬▬▬▬ 2mm malachite beads

▬ ▬ ▬ Lined blue lustre seed beads

·—·—·— Ceylon mint green seed beads

—·—·— Round transparent light blue seed beads

············ Translucent round lime seed beads

▬ ▬ ▬ Translucent round sky blue seed beads

— — — Transparent light tan AB seed beads

················ Lined light blue seed beads

– – – – Transparent crystal AB seed beads

▬ ▬ ▬ Transparent light tan AB seed beads

Fig. B - Couching
Use this technique to attach any bead with a hole that's too tiny for a needle.

Step 1 - String the beads on matching color beading thread. Lay the strung beads where you want to attach them. Thread a needle with the same thread. Bring up the needle between the first two beads. Loop the thread around the stringing thread, then bring the needle back through the foundation between the same two beads. Pull the thread snug.

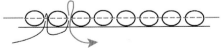

Step 2 - Continue, bringing the needle up and down after the second bead.

Step 3 - Continue to attach between the third and fourth beads.

Fig. C - Backstitching

Step 1 - Bring the needle up through the foundation in front of the bead (A). Pass the needle through the bead, then down through the foundation behind the bead (B).

Step 2 - Pull the thread snug. Sew the next bead, bringing up the needle in front of the bead (C) and back down (A).

Step 3 - Continue to sew beads.

Step 4 - To align the beads, bring the needle up at the end of the last bead and back through all of the beads.

continued from page 52

Finish:

1. Using small sharp scissors, carefully trim away the excess beading foundation. Be careful not to cut any of the threads.

2. Lay the beaded piece on the synthetic suede. Draw around the edge with a pencil.

3. Mark the position for the split rings. Poke a pin through the synthetic suede at each marked point and mark the other side. Sew the split rings in place with gold color thread on the opposite side from the outline. (You will not be able to sew them on after the ultrasuede is glued in place.)

4. To form one antenna, thread a sapphire 4mm bicone crystal on a thin 2-1/2" head pin, followed by alternating lined blue lustre and frost mint green seed beads (20 beads in all). See Fig.

D. Repeat the process to make a second one. Twist the head pins together tightly just below the beads and form the ends into loose flat coils. (The coils will provide good contact with the glue in the next step.)

5. Use the plastic knife to generously spread a layer of waterbase non-toxic super glue over the back of the piece. Be sure to cover all of the threads, especially around the edges. Lay the ends of the antennae in place, pressing the twisted coils of the wire firmly into the glue. Lay the beaded piece on the synthetic suede backing, aligning the edges of the beaded piece with the pencil outline on the ultrasuede. Press firmly over the entire piece for good contact. Let dry overnight.

6. Glue the pin back in place with the non-toxic super glue. Let dry thoroughly. ❏

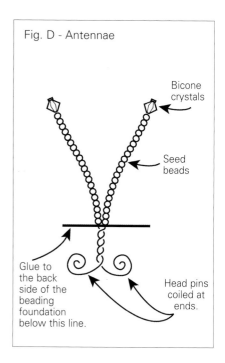

Fig. D - Antennae

Bicone crystals

Seed beads

Glue to the back side of the beading foundation below this line.

Head pins coiled at ends.

the rope

When determining how long to make the rope, consider what you will be wearing, e.g., if you wear it over a turtleneck sweater, you will need extra length to fit around the turtleneck. If you wear it with a collared shirt, you will also need extra length. With a jewel neck, it will hang straight from the neck and you will need less length for the butterfly to be hanging at the same level.

Each end of the rope is finished with the hook end of a lobster clasp (the part that looks like the lobster's claw). The clasp ends can be hooked to the loops sewn on the back of the brooch or hooked together so the rope may be worn without the brooch.

BEADING SUPPLIES

24 oval malachite beads, 4x6mm
10 faceted rondelle malachite beads, 8x4mm
6 round chryophase beads, 6mm
Malachite chips
2 small lobster clasps
Beading wire, .018
4 crimp beads

TOOLS & OTHER SUPPLIES

Wire cutters
Crimping pliers

INSTRUCTIONS

Start:

1. Determine how long you want your rope to be and cut a piece of beading wire about 4" longer. (For a 32" rope, use a 36" piece of beading wire.)

2. Thread two crimp beads on the wire, then thread the wire through the loop on the lobster clasp and back through the two crimp beads, leaving a 2" tail. Position the crimp beads snug against the ring on the clasp. Crimp them with crimping pliers.

String the Beads:

1. On the wire, place three rice-shaped malachite beads, one faceted rondelle malachite bead, one rice-shaped malachite bead, five malachite chips,

and three round chryophase beads.

2. Repeat the following sequence four times: Eight malachite chips, one rice-shaped malachite bead, one faceted rondelle malachite bead, and one rice-shaped malachite bead.

3. At this point, your strand should be about 9" long. This sequence will be repeated at the other end (another 9"). String enough malachite chips to make up the remainder of the length of the rope.

4. Repeat step 2 in reverse.

5. Repeat step 1 in reverse.

Finish:

1. Chips are, by their nature, uneven in size and shape. Smooth the strand with your hands to be sure that the chips are as close as possible to one another before you attach the other part of the clasp.

2. Thread two crimp beads on the wire. Thread the wire through the loop on the other side of the lobster clasp, then back through the crimp beads. Pull the wire snug, then crimp the crimp beads with crimping pliers. Carefully trim the wire tails. ❏

SUNSHINE JASPER
worry beads key chain

Fidgeting with or swinging a strand of worry beads can take your mind off your troubles and relieve stress. This key chain features leopard-skin jasper beads, which are thought to bring serenity and mental clarity. The pewter sun charm acts as a weight on the end of the strand.

Designed by Patty Cox

BEADING SUPPLIES

9 round leopard-skin jasper beads, 8mm
10 round hematite beads, 4mm
Silver cobra key chain
2 silver crimp beads
Pewter charm - Sun with thin face
Beading wire, .014

TOOLS & OTHER SUPPLIES

Wire cutters
Crimping tool

INSTRUCTIONS

Length: 6"

1. Cut 12" of bead stringing wire. Thread a crimp bead on one end. Thread the wire end through the small ring on the key chain, then back through the crimp bead, leaving a 1" tail. Crimp bead.
2. Thread a 4mm hematite and an 8mm jasper on the wire and over the wire tail. Repeat eight more times, ending with a 4mm hematite bead and a crimp bead.
3. Thread the wire end through the loop on the sun charm, then back through the crimp bead and several beads. Pull wire taut. Crimp bead. Cut wire tail. ❑

CALCITE & CARNELIAN DUO
necklace & earrings

A calcite disc and carnelian chips are combined with carved rectangular beads and tortoiseshell for an earthy, natural look. Carnelian is believed to improve one's sense of touch; calcite is believed to improve one's understanding of nature.

Designed by Patty Cox

BEADING SUPPLIES

1 honey calcite disc, 35mm

30" strand of carnelian bead chips

Yellow matte seed beads, size 11/0

11 golden carved rectangle beads, 8x12mm

31 round tortoiseshell beads, 6mm

1 gold spring ring clasp and eyelet, 7mm

5 gold crimp beads

3 gold head pins, 1-1/2"

2 gold ear wires

Beading wire, .014, flexible type

TOOLS & OTHER SUPPLIES

Wire cutters

Crimping tool

Roundnose pliers

INSTRUCTIONS

Make the Sides:

1. Cut two 36" lengths of beading wire.
2. Thread 2" of yellow matte seed beads on the center of one piece of wire. Wrap the wire through the center of the disc. Bring the wire ends together. Thread a 6mm tortoiseshell bead on both wires next to the seed beads. Add an 8x12mm gold rectangle bead and another 6mm tortoiseshell bead.
3. Separate the wires. Thread 1" of carnelian chip beads on each wire strand. Bring wire ends together. Thread a 6mm tortoiseshell bead on both wires, then an 8x12mm gold rectangle bead, and another 6mm tortoiseshell bead.
4. Separate the wires. Thread 1" of yellow matte seed beads on each wire. Bring the wire ends together. Thread a 6mm tortoiseshell bead on both wires, then an 8x12mm gold rectangle bead, and another 6mm tortoiseshell bead. Repeat steps 3 and 4.
5. Separate the wires. Thread 1" of carnelian chip beads on each wire strand. Bring the wire ends together. Thread a 6mm tortoiseshell bead on both wires. Separate the wires.
6. Thread 3" carnelian bead chips on each wire. Bring the wire ends together. Thread a 6mm tortoiseshell bead and a crimp bead on both wires. Thread both wire ends through half of the spring ring clasp, then back through crimp bead and tortoiseshell bead. Pull wires taut. Crimp the bead.
7. Thread wire ends back through several chip beads. Cut wire ends.
8. Repeat steps 2 through 7, using the second piece of wire, to make the second side of the necklace.

Make the Center Drop:

1. On an eye pin, thread a 6mm tortoiseshell bead and 1/2" to 3/4" of carnelian chip beads. Cut the end of the eye pin 3/8" from the beads. Using roundnose pliers, form a loop in the wire end.
2. Repeat the process to make three eye pin dangles.
3. Cut 10" of beading wire. Thread 2" of yellow matte seed beads on the center of the wire. Wrap the wire through the center of the calcite disc. Bring wire ends together.
4. Thread a 6mm tortoiseshell bead on both wires next to the seed beads. Add an 8x12mm gold rectangle bead and another 6mm tortoiseshell bead.
5. Thread the wire ends through the top loops of the three eye pins, then back through a crimp bead. Pull wires taut. Crimp bead.
6. Thread the wire ends back through the tortoiseshell and rectangular beads. Cut wire ends.

EARRINGS

1. On a 6" piece of wire, add 2" carnelian bead chips. Bring wire ends together to form a loop.
2. Thread a 6mm tortoiseshell bead and a crimp bead on both wires. Thread wires through ear wire, then back through the crimp bead and tortoiseshell bead. Pull wires taut. Crimp bead and cut wire ends.
3. Repeat steps 1 and 2 to make the other earring. ❏

CRYSTAL ENLIGHTENMENT
necklace & ear chains

This three-strand necklace features fluorite beads of various sizes and colors. Faceted glass beads add variety and sparkle. Wear this necklace when you are entering into stressful situations to attain serenity.

Designed by Patty Cox

BEADING SUPPLIES

40 (approx.) round fluorite beads, 8mm
50 (approx.) round fluorite beads, 6mm
25 (approx.) round fluorite beads, 4mm
10 (approx.) round fluorite beads, 3mm
2 pkgs. faceted Czech crystal or glass beads, 6mm (14/pkg.)
1 pkg. faceted Czech crystal or glass beads, 4mm (22/pkg.)
Sterling silver round beads, 2mm
1 silver 12mm 3-hole clasp
2 silver head pins, 1"
2 sterling silver ear chains
6 - silver crimp beads
2-1/4 yds. beading wire, .014

TOOLS & OTHER SUPPLIES

Wire cutters
Roundnose pliers

INSTRUCTIONS

Necklace length: 20"
The necklace is made with a silver bead between each fluorite bead and faceted Czech glass bead. Close the clasp when attaching the strands to the end of the clasp.

Make the 20" Outer Strand:

1. Cut a 30" piece of beading wire. Thread a silver crimp bead on the wire end. Thread the wire end through the outer clasp hole, then back through the crimp bead, leaving a 1" tail. Crimp bead.
2. Stringing the first beads over the wire tail, string the beads in this order, placing a silver bead between each fluorite and faceted Czech glass bead: 3mm round, 4mm round, 6mm round, 8mm round, 6mm faceted, 8mm round, 6mm round, 8mm round, 6mm faceted, 6mm round, 8mm round, 6mm faceted, two 6mm round, 8mm round, 6mm faceted, two 8mm round, 6mm faceted, three 8mm round, 6mm faceted, two 8mm round, 6mm faceted, and the three center front beads - all 8mm.
3. Repeat the sequence in reverse, except for the center beads, to make the other half of the outer strand, ending with a silver bead and a crimp bead.
4. Thread the wire end through the outer clasp hole on the opposite end of the clasp. Pull wires taut. Crimp bead. Thread wire end back through several beads. Cut the wire tail.

Make the 17" Middle Strand:

1. Cut a 27" piece of beading wire. Thread a silver crimp bead on the wire end. Thread the wire end through the center clasp hole, then back through the crimp bead, leaving a 1" tail. Crimp bead.
2. Stringing the first beads over the wire tail, string the beads in this order, placing a silver bead between each fluorite bead and faceted Czech glass bead: 3mm round, two 4mm round, 4mm faceted, three 6mm round, 4mm faceted, two 6mm round, 4mm faceted, three 6mm round, 6mm faceted, 6mm round, 8mm round, 6mm faceted, 6mm round, 8mm round, 6mm round, 6mm faceted, 8mm round, 6mm round, 6mm faceted, and the three center front beads - 6mm, 8mm, 6mm.
3. Repeat the sequence in reverse, except for the center beads, to make the other half of the middle strand, ending with a silver bead and a crimp bead.
4. Thread the wire end through the middle clasp hole on the opposite end of the clasp. Pull wires taut. Crimp bead. Thread wire end back through several beads. Cut the wire tail.

Make the 14" Inside Strand:

1. Cut a 24" piece of beading wire. Thread a silver crimp bead on the wire end. Thread the wire end through the remaining (inside) clasp hole, then back through the crimp bead, leaving a 1" tail. Crimp bead.
2. Stringing the first beads over the wire tail, string the beads in this order, placing a silver bead between each fluorite bead and faceted Czech glass bead: 3mm round, two 4mm round, 4mm faceted, two 4mm round, 4mm faceted, two 4mm round, 4mm faceted, three 4mm round, 4mm faceted, two 6mm round, 4mm faceted, three 6mm round, 4mm faceted, two 6mm round, 4mm faceted, and the three center front beads - all 6mm.

3. Repeat the sequence in reverse, except for the center beads, to make the other half of the inside strand, ending with a silver bead and a crimp bead.

4. Thread the wire end through the inside clasp hole on the opposite end of the clasp. Pull wires taut. Crimp bead. Thread wire end back through several beads. Cut the wire tail.

EAR CHAINS

1. On a silver head pin, thread a silver bead, 4mm fluorite round, silver bead, 4mm faceted, silver bead, 3mm fluorite round, and silver bead.

2. Cut the head pin end 3/8" from the beads. Use roundnose pliers to form a loop at the end of the head pin. Attach the head pin loop to the ear chain loop.

3. Repeat steps 1 and 2 to make the other earring. ❑

MOONSTONE GODDESS
necklace & earrings

Wear this necklace to feel confident and calm. Wearing moonstone is believed to soothe stress and anxiety. Here, moonstone disc beads are combined with round beads and tube beads of cat's eye, which is believed to bestow confidence, and with antique silver charms.

Designed by Patty Cox

BEADING SUPPLIES

50 (approx.) moonstone flat disc beads, 6mm to 8mm

20 (approx.) cat's eye round beads, 4mm and 5mm

20 (approx.) cat's eye tube beads, 4x8mm

50 (approx.) antique silver round beads, 5mm

45 (approx.) clear matte bicone beads, 6mm

Copper seed beads, size 10/0

2 antique silver moon charms

4 antique silver swirl dangle charms

1 silver moon goddess charm, 35mm

1 antique silver toggle clasp

2 silver lever-back ear wires

Beading wire, .012

TOOLS & OTHER SUPPLIES

Wire cutters

Clamp *or* bead stopper

Crimping tool

INSTRUCTIONS

Necklace length: 25"

Start:

1. Cut two 1-yd. lengths of bead stringing wire. Thread a crimp bead on both wires. Wrap the wire ends around one side of the clasp, then back through the crimp bead, leaving a 1" tail. Crimp bead.
2. Thread a copper seed bead and a cat's eye tube bead over both wires. Separate the wires.

Make the Outer (Longer) Strand:

1. On the outer strand, thread a 5mm antique silver bead, copper seed, clear bicone, copper seed, 4mm round cat's eye, copper seed, clear bicone, and copper seed.
2. Add a 5mm antique silver bead, copper seed, moonstone, copper seed, 4mm round cat's eye, copper seed, bicone, copper seed, moonstone, copper seed. Repeat this sequence eight times, replacing the antique silver bead with a charm on the third, fifth, and seventh repeats, as shown in the photo.
3. Attach the center goddess charm by running the wire through a copper seed bead, a bicone, a copper seed, and the goddess charm. Thread the wire back through the beads.
4. To complete the outer strand, fol-

low the beading sequence in step 1 in reverse. Place a clamp or stop bead on the end while you string the inner strand.

Make the Inner (Shorter) Strand:

1. Thread a copper seed, cat's eye tube, copper seed, antique silver bead, copper seed, bicone, copper seed, moonstone, copper seed, bicone, copper seed, antique silver bead, copper seed. Repeat the sequence five times, ending with a copper seed, cat's eye tube, copper seed, antique silver bead, copper seed, bicone, copper seed, moonstone, copper seed, bicone, copper seed, 4mm round cat's eye, and copper seed.
2. Thread a bicone at the center. Repeat the beading sequence in reverse to complete the other half of the strand.

Finish:

1. Bring both wire ends together. Thread both wires though a cat's eye tube and a copper seed bead. Thread a crimp bead on both wires.
2. Wrap the wire ends around the other side of the clasp, then back through crimp bead and several beads. Pull wires taut. Crimp bead. Cut wire ends.

Continued on page 62

Fig. A   Fig. B

continued from page 60

EARRINGS

1. Cut two 7" lengths of bead stringing wire.
2. On one wire, thread a copper seed bead, cat's eye tube, copper seed, antique silver bead, copper seed, bicone, copper seed, antique silver bead, copper seed, 4mm round cat's eye, copper seed, antique silver bead, copper seed, moonstone disc, copper seed, antique silver bead, copper seed, 4mm round cat's eye, copper seed, and antique silver bead.
3. Run the wire back through the copper seed, bicone, copper seed, antique silver bead, copper seed, cat's eye tube, and copper seed. Thread a crimp bead on both wires. (Fig. A)
4. Wrap the wire ends around the loop of the earring wire, then back through the crimp bead and several beads. Pull wires taut. Crimp bead. Cut wire ends. (Fig. B)
5. Repeat steps 2 through 4 to make the other earring. ❑

CRAZY LACE
leather braid necklace

Crazy lace agates are believed to relieve emotional pain and improve stamina. This necklace showcases a single large natural stone hung on a braided leather cord that was wrapped with gold wire.

Designed by Kathi Bailey

BEADING SUPPLIES

1 large crazy lace agate natural stone, drilled for beading
2 copper beads, 6mm
1 gold bead, 8mm
1 long gold eye pin
1 set silver cap clasps
Leather cord - Black, brown, copper, 24" of each
1 yd. gold wire, 22mm

TOOLS & OTHER SUPPLIES

Needlenose pliers
Wire cutters
Scissors
White glue
Roundnose pliers

INSTRUCTIONS
Necklace length: 16"

1. Insert the eye pin through the agate stone. Add a 6mm copper bead, 8mm gold bead, and 6mm copper bead. Using roundnose pliers, make a loop in the end of the eye pin for hanging.
2. Align the leather cords and loosely knot them together 2" from one end. Braid the cords, leaving 2" unbraided at other end.
3. Find center of leather braid and the center of the gold wire. Run the wire through the loop on the end of the agate eye pin. Leave the ends of the wire free.
4. Starting at the center of the braid and the center of the wire, wrap the wire tightly - 12 to 15 wraps - around the center area of the leather braid, attaching the eye pin with the stone and beads securely. Continue, wrapping the rest of the braid loosely on both sides with wire. Use the photo as a guide.
5. Untie the knotted ends of the braid. Insert gold wire into the end of the braid and cut to 3/4".
6. Insert both ends into cap clasps and glue. Allow glue to dry. ❑

GOLDEN STRANDS
twisted necklace

The four twisted golden-hued strands that make up this necklace include beads of yellow jasper, and brown moonstone, for soothing stress and anxiety.

Designed by Kathi Bailey

BEADING SUPPLIES

19 yellow jasper beads, 10mm
14 brown moonstone beads, 8mm
10 brown moonstone beads, 6mm
9 bi-cone wood beads, 10mm
Gold bugle beads, size 3
Gold seed beads, size 6/0
1 gold lobster clasp
Cotton beading thread

TOOLS & OTHER SUPPLIES

Beading needle
Tweezers
Scissors
White glue
Bead board

INSTRUCTIONS

Necklace length: 26"

1. Cut four 36" strands of cotton thread.
2. Lay out the beads on the bead board as follows and bead each strand, leaving 2" of thread at each end.

Strand 1 - Start with 20 gold seed beads. Begin stringing pattern with one 10mm yellow jasper, 8 gold seed beads, one wood bead, 8 gold seed beads, one 10mm yellow jasper. Continue pattern 8 more times. End with 20 gold seed beads.

Strand 2 - Start with 20 gold seed beads then one 8mm brown moonstone. Begin the stringing pattern with 25 gold seed beads, one 8mm brown moonstone, one 10mm yellow jasper, one 8mm brown moonstone. Continue the stringing pattern 4 more times. Then end with 25 gold seed beads, one 8mm moonstone, and 20 gold seed beads.

Strand 3 - Start with 40 gold seed beads then one 6mm brown moonstone. Begin stringing pattern with 25 gold seed beads, one 6mm brown moonstone, one 10mm yellow jasper, one 6mm brown moonstone. Repeat this pattern three more times. End with 25 gold seed beads, one 6mm brown moonstone, and 40 gold seed beads.

Strand 4 - gold bugle beads.

3. Knot and glue the end of each strand.
4. Knot one end of all four strands together. Twist strands four to five times and knot the other end of all strands together.
5. Add an 8mm moonstone to the end of each strand before adding clasp.
6. Attach clasps to each end. Knot the threads and glue to secure. Allow glue to dry. ❏

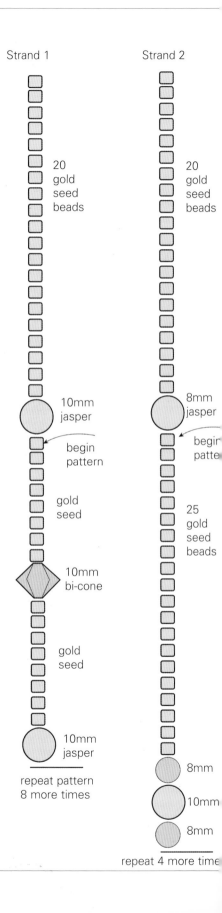

Strand 1

20 gold seed beads

10mm jasper

begin pattern

gold seed

10mm bi-cone

gold seed

10mm jasper

repeat pattern 8 more times

Strand 2

20 gold seed beads

8mm jasper

begin patte

25 gold seed beads

8mm

10mm

8mm

repeat 4 more time

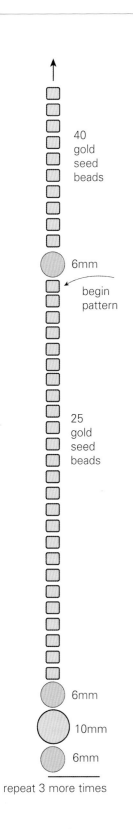

40
gold
seed
beads

6mm

begin
pattern

25
gold
seed
beads

6mm

10mm

6mm

repeat 3 more times

FAVORITE FLUORITE
pendant & earrings

Wear fluorite when you need to concentrate on the moment and clear your mind of stress. Here, the earthy colors of a sleek, tongue-shaped fluorite pendant and round fluorite beads in graduated sizes are accented with amethyst and gold seed beads.

Designed by Patty Cox

BEADING SUPPLIES

1 fluorite tongue-shaped pendant, 20x40mm

60 round fluorite beads, 3mm

24 round fluorite beads, 4mm

6 round fluorite beads, 6mm

Dark amethyst seed beads, size 11/0

Amethyst matte seed beads, size 6/0

Gold matte seed beads

1 gold toggle clasp

4mm gold jump rings

1 gold eye pin

6 gold crimp beads

Bead stringing wire, .012

TOOLS & OTHER SUPPLIES

Wire cutters

Roundnose pliers

Ruler

Clamp *or* bead stopper

INSTRUCTIONS

Necklace length: 25"

See Fig. A.

Prepare Pendant:

1. On an eye pin, thread a 6/0 amethyst matte bead, the tongue-shaped pendant, and another amethyst matte bead. Cut the end of the wire 3/8" from the last bead.

2. Form a loop in the end of the wire with roundnose pliers.

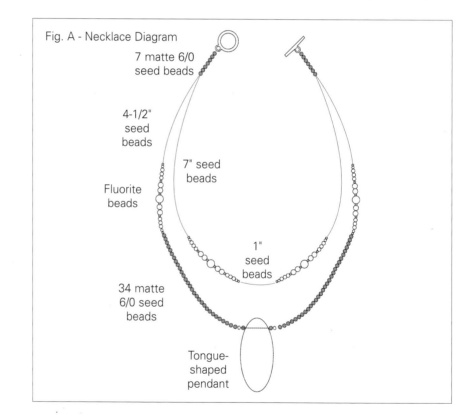

Fig. A - Necklace Diagram

7 matte 6/0 seed beads

4-1/2" seed beads

7" seed beads

Fluorite beads

1" seed beads

34 matte 6/0 seed beads

Tongue-shaped pendant

Start the Strands:

1. Cut two 1-yd. lengths of bead stringing wire. Thread a crimp bead on the ends of both wires. Wrap the wire ends around one side of the clasp, then back through the crimp bead, leaving a 1" tail. Crimp bead.

2. Thread seven 6/0 amethyst matte beads on both wires and over the wire tails. Separate the wires.

Make the Outer Strand:

1. On the outer (longer) strand, thread 4-1/2" of dark amethyst seed beads. Add a gold seed bead, five 3mm fluorite beads, a gold seed, two 4mm fluorite beads, a gold seed, 6mm fluorite, a gold seed, two 4mm fluorite, a gold seed, five 3mm fluorite, and a gold seed.

continued on page 68

continued from page 66

2. Thread 34 amethyst (6/0) matte beads on the wire, ending with a crimp bead.
3. Thread the wire end through the eye pin loop on the tongue-shaped pendant, then back through the crimp bead and seed several beads. Pull wire taut. Crimp bead. Cut wire end.
4. Repeat bead stringing sequence in reverse to make the other side of the outer strand. Use a clamp or bead stopper on the end of the strand to hold the beads in place.

Make the Inner Strand:
1. On the remaining wire, thread 7" of dark amethyst seed beads.
2. Add a gold seed bead, five 3mm fluorite beads, gold seed bead, two 4mm fluorite beads, gold seed bead, 6mm fluorite bead, gold seed bead, two 4mm fluorite beads, gold seed bead, five 3mm fluorite beads, and gold seed bead.
3. Add 1" of amethyst seed beads.
4. Repeat the beading sequence in step 2.
5. Add 7" dark amethyst seed beads to complete the strand.

Finish:
1. Bring the ends of both wires together. Thread seven 6/0 amethyst matte beads over both wires, ending with a crimp bead.
2. Thread both wires around the other side of the clasp, then back through the crimp bead and several beads. Pull wires taut. Crimp bead. Cut wire tails.

EARRINGS
1. Cut two 8" lengths of bead stringing wire.
2. On one wire, thread a gold seed bead, five 3mm fluorite beads, gold seed bead, two 4mm fluorite beads, gold seed bead, 6mm fluorite bead, gold seed bead, two 4mm fluorite beads, gold seed bead, five 3mm fluorite beads, and gold seed bead.
3. Bring both wire ends together. Thread both wires through a 6/0 amethyst matte bead and a crimp bead.
4. Fold wires around one ear wire loop, then back through the crimp bead and 6/0 bead. Pull wires taut. Crimp bead. Cut wire ends.
5. Repeat steps 2 through 4 to make the other earring. ❏

SERENITY
rose quartz & fluorite strand

This piece combines beads of rose quartz and fluorite, two stones believed to enhance serenity, gentleness, and calm. Elastic beading cord makes this an easy-on, easy-off piece and allows the stones to touch your skin. It can be used as a necklace, or twisted into several strands for a bracelet.

Designed by Kathi Bailey

BEADING SUPPLIES
34 rose quartz beads, 6mm
33 fluorite beads, 6mm
Rose seed beads, size 11/0
Elastic beading cord

TOOLS & OTHER SUPPLIES
Beading needle
Tweezers
Scissors
Beading glue

INSTRUCTIONS
Bracelet length: 20"

1. Cut 20" of elastic cord. Thread needle so that elastic is doubled. Knot the end.
2. String beads in this order: one rose quartz bead, one seed bead, one fluorite bead, one seed bead. Repeat to end - when you've used up all the beads or the bracelet is your desired length.
3. Knot and glue end. Knot ends together to make a continuous strand. Secure with glue. Let dry. ❏

RED BRANCHES & NUGGET
coral necklace & earrings

Red coral is said to calm and attune us to earth energies. Two forms of red coral - a round, textured nugget and polished bamboo branch-shaped beads - display the stone's subtle variations in color. They are combined with sections of silver chain to create a necklace that is both delicate and bold.

Designed by Patty Cox

BEADING SUPPLIES

1 coral nugget bead, 24x28x9mm

34 red bamboo branch-shaped coral beads

18 silver jump rings, 4mm

Silver lobster claw clasp

8 silver eye pins

2 silver head pins, 2"

1 silver bead cap, 5mm

1 silver bead cap, 9mm

2 silver ear wires

16" silver figaro necklace chain

TOOLS & OTHER SUPPLIES

Needlenose pliers

Roundnose pliers

Ruler

INSTRUCTIONS
Necklace length: 24"

Make the Coral Branch Sections:

1. Thread three branch-shaped coral beads on an eye pin. Cut the eye pin wire 3/8" from the last bead. (Photo 1)
2. Using roundnose pliers, form a loop in the end of the wire next to the last bead. (Photo 2) Repeat the process to make eight coral branch sections.

Make the Pendant:

1. On a head pin, thread a 5mm bead cap, the coral nugget bead, and an 8mm bead cap. Cut the head pin wire 3/8" from the last bead.
2. Using round nose pliers, form a loop in wire end.

Assemble the Necklace:

1. Cut the wire chain into six 1" sections and three 2" sections.
2. Attach the top loop of the coral nugget pendant to the center of one 2" section.
3. Attach a coral branch bead section on each side of the center chain with a jump ring - here's how: Open a jump ring from side to side. Attach ring to chain or eye pin. Close jump ring using needlenose pliers. (Photo 3)
4. On each side of the necklace, attach a 1" chain piece and a coral branch bead section with jump rings.
5. Add two more coral branch bead sections to each side with 1" pieces of chain between the bead sections with jump rings.
6. Attach one of the remaining 2" chain sections to each end of the necklace with jump rings.
7. Attach the ends of the chain to the clasp with jump rings.

EARRINGS

1. On a head pin, thread five branch-shaped coral beads.
2. Cut the head pin wire 3/8" from the last bead.
3. Using roundnose pliers, form a loop in the wire end.
4. Attach the head pin loop to the ear wire loop.
5. Repeat steps 1 through 4 to make the other earring. ❑

Photo 1 - Cut the eye pin 3/8" from the last bead.

Photo 2 - Use roundnose pliers to form a loop in the end of the wire.

Photo 3 - Use jump rings to join the bead sections and chains.

MARIPOSA MAGIC
necklace & earrings

Mariposite is a power stone for artists - it is said to stimulate self-expression. *Mariposa* is the Spanish word for butterfly. In this necklace, reminiscent of a western bolo string tie, Patty combined a maraposite disc and silver butterfly spacer beads with an array of colorful beads (amethyst, carnelian, jade, and yellow jasper, and glass). You can follow the written instructions or use Patty's idea to create your own artistic bead combination.

Designed by Patty Cox

BEADING SUPPLIES

1 green mariposite disc, 40mm

1 amethyst bicone bead, 12mm x 22mm

30 (approx.) round red bamboo coral beads, 4mm

20 (approx.) yellow jasper beads, 5mm

15 (approx.) jade round beads, 4mm

15 (approx.) carnelian chips

2 amethyst beads, 6mm

2 amethyst beads, 8mm

5 amethyst bicone beads, 8mm

Czech glass beads, gold assorted

Czech glass beads, green assorted

70 (approx.) silver daisy spacer beads

Amethyst matte seed beads, size 6/0

Dark amethyst seed beads, size 11/0

Teal matte AB seed beads

Opaque orange seed beads

Silver crimp beads

1 silver toggle clasp

5 antique silver butterfly spacer beads

Beading wire, .015

Beading wire, .012

necklace: 2 - 24" lengths .015 beading wire

fringe: 3 - 15" lengths .012 beading wire

earrings: each 3 - 7" lengths .012 beading wire

TOOLS & OTHER SUPPLIES

Wire cutters

Crimping tool

Beading board or shallow plastic cups

INSTRUCTIONS
Necklace length: 16"

Start:

Gather the various beads and arrange them on a beading board or in shallow plastic cups according to size and color, dividing them into groups by these categories:

- Warm-color smaller beads (reds and yellows - e.g., jasper, red coral, orange seed beads, carnelian chips)
- Green smaller beads (jade, teal seeds, etc.)
- Larger beads (amethyst bicone, larger glass beads)
- Novelty glass beads (e.g., teardrop shapes, leaves)
- Silver spacers
- Silver butterfly spacers

The instructions will direct you to use different categories of beads to make the necklace. How you combine them is a matter of personal choice - express yourself! Use the project photo as a guide.

Make the Choker:

1. Cut two 24" lengths of size .015 beading wire. Add a crimp bead over the ends of both wires. Slide the crimp bead down the wires about 3".

continued on page 74

continued from page 72

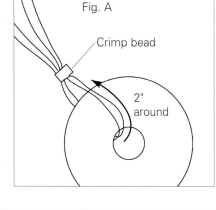

2. Add 2" of seed beads and small beads on each wire, making one wire with green beads and another with warm-colored beads. Wrap the beaded wires through the hole in the disc. Thread the wire ends back through the crimp bead. (Fig. A) Pull wires taut around the disc. Crimp bead.

3. Thread three larger beads with large holes on the wire ends to cover the crimp bead and wire tails.

4. Separate wires. Thread 1-3/4" seed beads and small beads on each wire. (Fig. B) Add green beads on one wire and orange and gold beads on the other wire.

5. Bring the wires together. Thread a 1" length with larger beads of various colors, including amethyst. Add silver spacers here and there as accents.

6. Separate the wires. Repeat steps 4 and 5 until you have a strand 16" long.

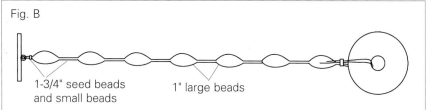

7. Finish with 1-3/4" of seed beads and small beads on each wire. Bring the wires together and attach the toggle part of the clasp. Add a crimp bead over both wires. Thread wires around the toggle loop, then back through the crimp bead and several seed beads. Pull wires taut. Crimp bead.

Make the Three-Strand Fringe:

See Fig. C.

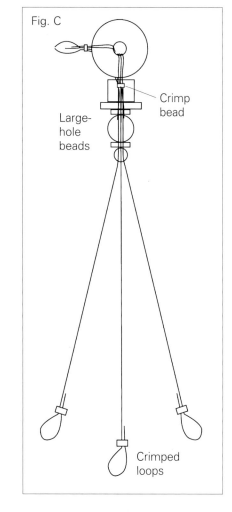

1. Cut three 15" lengths of size .012 bead stringing wire. Add a crimp bead over all the wires. Slide the crimp bead down the wires about 3". Add 2" of teal seed beads on two wires. Put 2" of orange seed beads on the other wire.

2. Wrap the beaded wires through the hole in the disc. Thread the wire ends back through the crimp bead. Pull wires taut around the disc. Crimp bead. Thread three to four large beads with large holes on the wire to cover the crimp bead and wire tails.

3. Add a variety of beads, silver spacers, and butterfly spacers on each wire, using warm-color and amethyst beads (large and small) on one wire and green beads (also large and small) on two wires. Near the end of each wire, add a crimp bead, then seven seed beads, a drop bead, and seven seed beads. Run wire tail back through crimp beads and several beads. Pull wire taut, but not tight so the wire will dangle. Crimp bead. Cut wire tail.

4. Thread toggle clasp through the hole in the disc to close the choker.

EARRINGS

1. Cut three 7" lengths of size .012 beading wire. Thread a crimp bead over all three wires. Wrap the wire ends around the loop of an ear wire, then back through the crimp bead. Crimp bead.

2. Thread a 4mm green glass, a 10mm green matte oval and a 4mm green glass bead over all wires and wire tails. Separate wires.

3. Add beads on each wire. Make two wires with green beads. Fill one with yellow, gold, and amethyst beads.

4. Near the end of each wire, add a crimp bead, then seven seed beads, a drop bead, and seven seed beads. Run the wire tail back through the crimp beads and several beads. Pull wire taut, but not tight so the wire will dangle. Crimp bead. Cut wire tail.

5. Repeat steps 1 through 4 to make the other earring. ❑

RIPPLES OF CONTENTMENT
amethyst brooch

Here, natural amethyst stones are combined with pure white pearl seed beads on a rippled polymer clay brooch. Create this pin and you will be creating contentment for the wearer.

Designed by Kathi Bailey

BEADING SUPPLIES

9 small natural amethyst stones

Pearl seed beads, size 11/0

TOOLS & OTHER SUPPLIES

Polymer clay, 1/4 oz. *each* - Gold, silver

Polymer clay knife

1 pin back

Tweezers

Scissors

Beading glue

Pattern (actual size)

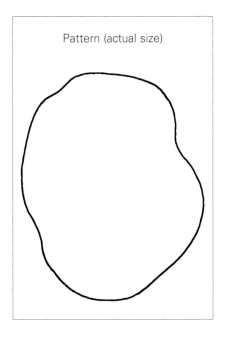

INSTRUCTIONS

Size: 2-1/2" x 2"

1. Knead and roll each block of clay into cylinders. Twist the cylinders together and knead again lightly. Roll into 1-1/2" ball and flatten with your fingers to make a sheet about 1/4" thick.
2. Using the pattern provided, use a knife to cut out the shape. Crumple the clay slightly to create a rippled effect.
3. Press amethyst stones in a random pattern on the clay surface.
4. Bake following manufacturer's instructions and allow to cool.
5. Glue seed beads randomly around the stones. Use tweezers to place the seed beads. Let dry.
6. Attach pin back with glue. Let dry. ❏

PEARLS OF THE SEA
twisted necklace & earrings

The colors of the sea are combined with natural pearls in this elegant necklace. Pearls are thought to symbolize purity, spirituality, and virtue. You will feel less stressful when you wear this necklace.

Designed by Patty Cox

BEADING SUPPLIES

3 strands, each 16", aqua freshwater pearls, 8mm

36" strand synthetic blue topaz bead chips

Czech glass seed bead mix, sea colors

Czech clear glass bead mix

5 turquoise glass beads, 6mm

1 turquoise glass bead, 8mm

2 silver lever-back ear wires

2 silver split rings, 9mm

1 silver hook-type clasp

2 silver split rings, 9mm

5 silver eye pins

1 silver head pin

Beading wire, .015

TOOLS & OTHER SUPPLIES

Wire cutters

Crimping tool

Roundnose pliers

INSTRUCTIONS
Necklace length: 18"

Make the Strands:

1. Cut two 2-1/2 yd. lengths of beading wire. Crimp a temporary crimp bead on one end of each wire.

2. Thread 1 yd. of blue topaz chips on one wire. Add 1 yd. clear seed beads on the same wire, ending with a silver crimp bead.

3. Cut the temporary crimp bead from the end of the wire. Thread wire ends through a crimp bead and a few seed beads, forming a circle of beads. (Fig. A) Pull wires taut. Crimp bead. Cut wire ends.

4. Repeat the process with the second wire to make a strand with 1 yd. aqua pearls and 1 yd. clear beads.

Assemble the Necklace:

1. Cut two 4" pieces of beading wire and set aside.

2. Hold both beaded strands together, aligning the crimp beads. Hold each end of the strands with your fingers and pull and twist the strands into a single, tight twist. (Fig. B)

continued on page 78

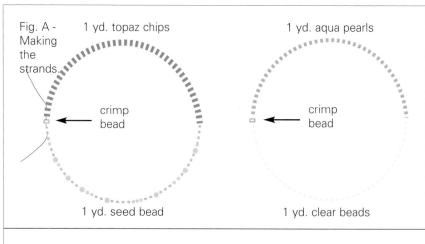

Fig. A - Making the strands.

1 yd. topaz chips

1 yd. aqua pearls

crimp bead

crimp bead

1 yd. seed bead

1 yd. clear beads

Fig. B - Twisting the strands.

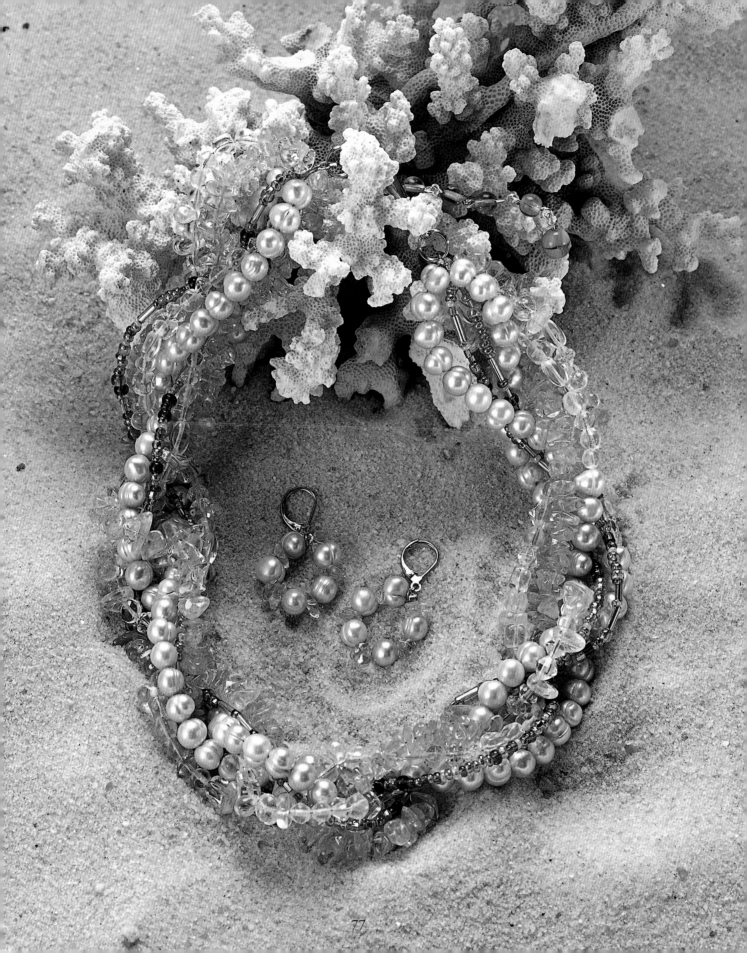

Fig. C -
Bring ends
together
and allow
strands to
fall and
twist
together.

continued from page 76

3. Quickly bring the ends together and allow the middles of the strands to drop and twist together (Fig. C).
4. Thread the 4" piece of beading wire through one looped end. Add a crimp bead on each end of the wire, then thread the wire ends through each crimp bead. Pull wires tightly, securing the ends of the looped strands. Crimp beads. (You've made a small loop of beading wire.) Trim the wire. Repeat the process on the other end of the looped strands, using the other piece of wire.
5. Attach a split ring to each of the beading wire loops (Fig. D).
6. Attach the clasp to the split rings.
7. To make the necklace extension, thread an eye pin through a 6mm turquoise glass bead. Trim the eye pin 3/8" from the bead. Bend the straight end into a loop with roundnose pliers. Connect a second eye pin through the loop. Add a bead to the second eye pin. Trim the straight end 3/8" from the bead. Bend into a loop. Continue making beaded chain, using five 6mm beads and ending with an 8mm bead threaded on a head pin (Fig E). ❑

Fig. D - Anchor the ends with split rings.

Fig. E - Adding the clasp and extension beads.

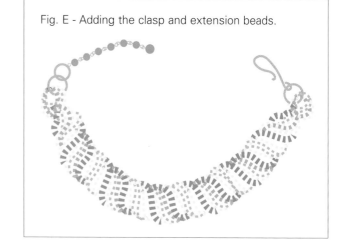

EARRINGS

1. Cut two 6" lengths of beading wire.
2. On one wire, alternately thread 5 aqua pearls and 5 topaz bead chips. (Use two chips instead of one if the chips are very small.)
3. Thread a crimp bead on the end of the wire. Thread the beginning of the wire through the crimp bead and several beads. Pull wires taut. Crimp bead. Cut wire tails.
4. Attach an ear wire loop to the beaded loop at the crimp bead.
5. Repeat steps 2 through 4 to make the second earring. ❑

Caring for Pearls

• Wear them often - your natural body oils help to keep them from drying out.

• Avoid contact with hair spray and perfume, which can dry and damage pearls.

• To clean them, wipe with a soft, damp cloth.

• Store pearls in a soft cloth bag.

LAPIS & HAND OF FATIMA
choker & earrings

The necklace and earrings include lapis beads and five Hand of Fatima charms. The Hand of Fatima is an ancient symbol of protection. Lapis lazuli is a stone thought to protect against physical harm. With these two protective elements combined in one necklace, this is sure to be a piece of jewelry that wards off evil and harm.

Designed by Patty Cox

Pictured on page 81

BEADING SUPPLIES

60 (approx.) lapis lazuli beads, 6mm

Dark blue glass beads, 2mm

16 dark blue glass beads, 4mm

Blue-gray seed beads

Silver matte seed beads

5 antique silver hand of fatima charms

10 antique silver daisy spacer beads

Antique silver metal bead mix

1 antique silver toggle clasp

24 antique silver bead caps

10 silver head pins, 2"

2 silver eye pins, 2"

2 silver ear wires

5 silver jump rings

2 silver crimp beads

Optional: 2 silver bead tips (to cover the thread knots)

Beading thread

Beading wire, .012

TOOLS & OTHER SUPPLIES

Beading needle

Wire cutters

Roundnose pliers

Clamp

Scissors

Beading glue

INSTRUCTIONS
Necklace length: 15"

Make the Dangles:

1. On a head pin, thread a silver matte seed bead, 2mm blue, bead cap, 6mm lapis, bead cap, 4mm blue, silver matte seed bead, and a 2mm blue bead. (Fig. A)
2. Cut the head pin wire 3/8" from the last bead. Form a loop in the end of the wire, using roundnose pliers.
3. Repeat steps 1 and 2 to make 10 head pin dangles in all.
4. Attach a jump ring through the top loop of three hand of fatima charms.

String the Strand:

1. Cut 24" of beading wire. Thread a crimp bead on one end of the wire. Thread the wire end through one side of the clasp, then back through the crimp bead, leaving a 1" tail. Crimp bead.
2. Thread beads on the wire, threading the first five beads over the wire and wire tail: 4mm blue, 6mm lapis, metal bead, 6mm lapis, and head pin dangle. (Fig. B)
3. Add a 6mm lapis, metal bead, 6mm lapis, metal bead, 6mm lapis, and head pin dangle. Repeat three times ending with a hand of fatima charm instead of a head pin dangle.

continued on next page

continued from page 79

4. Add a 6mm lapis, metal bead, 6mm lapis, metal bead, 6mm lapis, head pin dangle, 6mm lapis, and metal bead.

5. Add the center hand of fatima charm.

6. Repeat step 4 in reverse, then step 3 in reverse. Add the beads listed in step 2 in reverse to finish the other half of the necklace.

7. Clamp the wire end while adding the bead scallops.

Add the Bead Scallops:

See Fig. C.

1. Thread a beading needle with 1 yd. of beading thread. Tie one end over the crimp bead and wire at the end of the necklace.

2. Run the needle through the first five beads and head pin dangle.

3. Bring out the needle at the lapis bead. Thread seven silver gray seed beads, a lapis bead, and seven silver gray seed beads on the needle and thread. Pass the needle through the next lapis bead, then exit. (Fig. C)

4. Thread seven silver gray seed beads, a 2mm blue, a silver daisy spacer, a 2mm blue, and seven silver gray seed beads on the needle and thread. Pass the needle through the next lapis bead, the head pin of the dangle, and lapis bead. Exit after the lapis bead. (Fig. C)

5. Repeat steps 3 and 4, making bead scallops to hang off each silver bead, to the end of the necklace.

Finish:

1. Thread a crimp bead on the wire end. Thread the wire end around the other side of the toggle clasp, then back through the crimp bead and several beads. Pull wire taut. Crimp bead. Cut wire end.

2. Knot the needle and thread around the ending crimp bead, then pass back through several beads. Cut the thread tail. Dot knots with glue.

3. *Option:* Cover knots with bead tips.

EARRINGS

1. On a head pin, thread a silver matte seed bead, 2mm blue, bead cap, 6mm lapis, bead cap, 4mm blue, silver matte seed bead and a 2mm blue bead.

2. Cut the head pin wire 3/8" from the last bead. Form a loop in the wire end, using roundnose pliers.

3. Repeat steps 1 and 2 to make two pin dangles in all.

4. Attach a jump ring in the top loop of each of two hand of fatima charms. Attach one to the bottom loop of each eye pin dangle.

5. Attach top loop of each dangle to an ear wire. ❑

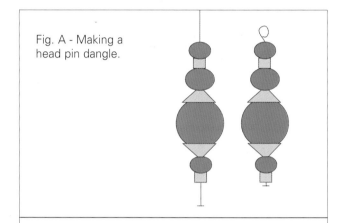

Fig. A - Making a head pin dangle.

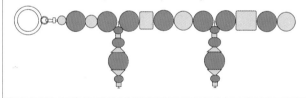

Fig. B - Attaching the head pin dangles to the necklace.

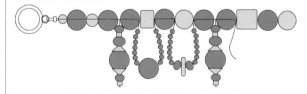

Fig. C - Adding bead scallops between lapis beads on the necklace.

SPHERES & CUBES
onyx choker & earrings

This necklace is a sophisticated combination of three sizes of round black onyx beads and silver cube beads. Wear this piece when you need to be grounded so that you can make good decisions. This can only result in happiness and good fortune.

Designed by Patty Cox

BEADING SUPPLIES

29 black onyx round beads, 8mm

29 black onyx round beads, 6mm

77 black onyx round beads, 4mm

32 silver-plated cube beads, 4mm

1 sterling silver S-hook clasp

2 silver crimp beads

27 sterling silver fancy head pins

140 (approx.) sterling silver plated beads, 2.4mm

2 sterling silver ear wires

2 silver bead caps

Beading thread

Beading wire

TOOLS & OTHER SUPPLIES

Beading needle

Thread

Wire cutters

Crimping tool

Roundnose pliers

Ruler

Beading glue

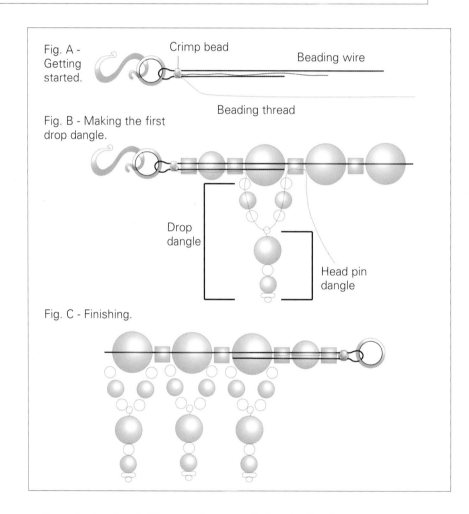

Fig. A - Getting started.

Crimp bead

Beading wire

Beading thread

Fig. B - Making the first drop dangle.

Drop dangle

Head pin dangle

Fig. C - Finishing.

INSTRUCTIONS
Necklace length: 14"

Make the Head Pin Dangles:

1. On a fancy head pin, thread a 4mm onyx, a 2.4mm silver bead, and a 6mm onyx.
2. Cut off the end of the head pin 3/8" from the last bead. Use roundnose pliers to form a loop in the head pin wire.
3. Repeat steps 1 and 2 to make 25 head pin dangles in all.

String the Beads:

1. Cut 24" of beading wire. Thread a crimp bead on one end. Fold the wire end around one side of the clasp, then back through the crimp bead. Crimp bead. (Fig. A)

2. Cut 30" of beading thread. Knot one end securely around the crimp bead and wire. Thread the other end through the eye of a beading needle. (Fig. A)

3. Thread a silver cube, 6mm onyx, 8mm onyx, and silver cube over the wire, wire tail, thread, and thread tail. Separate the thread from the wire. Place an 8mm onyx and a silver cube on the wire.

4. To make the drop dangle, on the thread add a 2.4 silver bead, 4mm onyx, 2.4mm silver bead, 1 head pin dangle, 2.4mm silver bead, 4mm onyx, 2.4mm silver bead. Put the needle and thread through the silver cube on the necklace wire. (Fig. B)

5. Continue to bead the necklace, alternating 8mm onyx and silver cubes on the wire and adding drop dangles on beading thread (step 4) between the silver cubes.

continued on page 84

83

continued from page 83
Finish:
1. After you have attached all 25 head pin dangles, finish the necklace with a 6mm onyx, a silver cube, and a crimp bead. (Fig. C)
2. Fold the wire around the other side of the clasp, then back through the crimp bead. Thread the wire tail back through several beads. Pull wire taut. Crimp bead.
3. Run the threaded needle through the end beads. Knot the thread end over the crimp bead and around the beading wire. Run the threaded needle back through several beads.

4. Add a dot of glue and a silver bead cap over the crimp bead and knotted thread. Repeat on other crimp bead.

EARRINGS
1. On a fancy head pin, thread a 4mm onyx, 2.4mm silver bead, 6mm onyx, silver cube, and 8mm onyx.
2. Cut the end of the head pin 3/8" from the last bead. Use roundnose pliers to form a loop in the end of the head pin wire.
3. Attach the head pin loop to an ear wire loop.
4. Repeat steps 1 through 3 to make the other earring. ❏

LUMINOUS PROTECTION
quartz & pearls necklace & ear chains

Here oblong ruby quartz beads are combined with crystal pearls and gold spacer beads.
Wear this piece if you want to add passion and vitality to your life.

Designed by Patty Cox

BEADING SUPPLIES
8 ruby quartz beads, 36x12mm
3 crystal beads with pearl finish, 15mm
9 crystal beads with pearl finish, 12mm
4 crystal beads with pearl finish, 10mm
4 crystal beads with pearl finish, 8mm
18 gold drum bead spacers, 7mm
1 gold hook and eye clasp
2 gold ear chains
2 gold head pins, 2"
2 gold crimp beads
8 gold seed beads
2 gold beads, 6mm
Beading wire, .018

TOOLS & OTHER SUPPLIES
Wire cutters • Crimping tool
Roundnose pliers • Ruler

INSTRUCTIONS
Necklace length: 21"

1. Cut 30" of beading wire. Thread a crimp bead on one wire end. Wrap the wire end around one side of the clasp, then back through the crimp bead, leaving a 1" tail. Crimp bead.
2. Thread a 6mm gold bead, 8mm crystal, seed bead, 10mm crystal, and seed bead on wire and wire tail.
3. Add a 12mm crystal, gold drum bead, ruby quartz bead, and gold drum bead. Repeat this sequence seven times.

4. Thread the wire end with a 12mm crystal, seed bead, 10mm crystal, seed bead, 8mm crystal, 6mm gold bead, and a crimp bead.
5. Thread wire end through the other side of the clasp, then back through the crimp bead and several beads. Pull wires taut. Crimp bead. Cut wire tail.

EAR CHAINS
1. On a head pin, thread a seed bead, 10mm crystal, gold drum bead, 8mm crystal, and seed bead. Cut wire 3/8" from bead.
2. Make a loop in the end of the wire using roundnose pliers.
3. Attach ear chain loop to head pin loop.
4. Repeat steps 1 through 3 to make the other ear chain. ❏

EARTH & SEA
jasper & pearl set

In this necklace, the natural, earthy colors of poppy jasper and picture jasper are combined with the healing, peaceful sea energy of mother of pearl. Your fears will float away when you wear this piece.

Designed by Patty Cox

BEADING SUPPLIES
11 poppy jasper nuggets, 15x12mm
40 picture jasper beads, 8mm
63 mother of pearl nuggets
64 coconut wood wheels, 6mm
Rust orange seed beads, size 8/0
Gold heishi spacers, 5mm
1 gold toggle clasp
2 gold filled fish hook ear wires
2 gold head pins
4 gold crimp beads
Beading wire, .015

TOOLS & OTHER SUPPLIES
Wire cutters
Crimping tool
Clamp
Roundnose pliers

INSTRUCTIONS
Necklace length: 20"

Start:
1. Cut two 30" lengths of beading wire. Thread a crimp bead over both wires. Thread wire ends around one side of the toggle clasp, then back through the crimp bead. Crimp bead.
2. Thread a coconut bead over both wires. Separate the wires.

Make the Outer (Longer) Strand:
1. On outer wire, thread five rust seed beads.
2. Thread a coconut bead, heishi spacer, 8mm picture jasper, heishi spacer, coconut bead, three mother of pearl nuggets, coconut bead, heishi spacer, 8mm picture jasper, heishi spacer, coconut, three rust seed beads. Repeat this sequence (step 2) one time.
3. Thread a coconut bead, heishi spacer, 8mm picture jasper, heishi spacer, coconut bead, three mother of pearl nuggets, coconut bead, heishi spacer, 8mm picture jasper, heishi spacer, coconut, and poppy jasper nugget. Repeat this sequence (step 3) two times (for a total of three times).
4. Repeat step 3 in reverse, then step 2 in reverse, then step 1 to make the other side of the outer strand. Clamp while you bead the inner strand.

Make the Inner (Shorter) Strand:
1. On the inner wire, thread five rust seed beads.
2. Thread a coconut bead, heishi spacer, 8mm picture jasper, heishi spacer, coconut bead, three mother of pearl nuggets, coconut bead, heishi spacer, 8mm picture jasper, heishi spacer, coconut, three rust seed beads. Repeat this sequence (step 2) two times (for a total of three).
3. Thread a coconut bead, heishi spacer, 8mm picture jasper, heishi spacer, coconut bead, three mother of pearl nuggets, coconut bead, heishi spacer, 8mm picture jasper, heishi spacer, coconut, and poppy jasper nugget. Repeat this sequence once (for total of two times).
4. At the center of the strand, thread an 8mm picture jasper, heishi spacer, coconut, three mother of pearl nuggets, coconut, heishi spacer, and 8mm picture jasper.
5. Repeat step 3 in reverse, then step 2 in reverse, then step 1 to complete the other half of the inner strand.

Finish:
1. Bring wire ends from both strands together. Thread a coconut bead and a crimp bead over both strands.
2. Wrap the wires through the other side of the toggle clasp, then back through the crimp bead and several beads. Pull wires taut. Crimp bead.

EARRINGS
1. On a head pin, thread a coconut bead, poppy jasper nugget, 8mm picture jasper, heishi spacer, coconut bead, and three mother of pearl nuggets.
2. Cut the top of the head pin 3/8" from the last bead.
3. Form a loop in the wire end using roundnose pliers.
4. Attach an ear wire loop to the head pin loop.
5. Repeat steps 1 through 4 to make the other earring. ❑

EARTH & SKY
turquoise necklace & earrings

This lovely necklace and earring set is a twist on the traditional. Beautiful beads of turquoise are combined with sterling silver for a time honored design, with the glass beads adding an updated look. Wear this necklace to "shoo" away evil and negative energy. Wear this when you need spiritual uplifting.

Designed by Patty Cox

BEADING SUPPLIES

95 (approx.) turquoise wheels, 6-8mm

25 (approx.) turquoise tubes, approx. 5x14mm

45 (approx.) round blue glass beads, 6mm

8 round blue glass beads, 4mm

1 sterling silver S-hook clasp

2 sterling silver ear wires

2 sterling silver fancy head pins

90 sterling silver Rococo round spacers, 4mm

3 sterling silver seed beads

2 crimp beads

Beading wire, .015

TOOLS & OTHER SUPPLIES

Wire cutters

Crimping tool

Roundnose pliers

Clamp

INSTRUCTIONS
Necklace length: 25"

Start:

1. Cut two 30" lengths beading wire. Thread a crimp bead on both wires. Wrap wire ends around one loop of the clasp, then back through the crimp bead, leaving 1" wire tails. Crimp bead.
2. On both wires, thread a 4mm blue glass bead.
3. On both wires, thread a silver spacer, one 4mm tube, silver spacer, 6mm blue glass, silver spacer, four turquoise wheels, silver spacer, and 6mm blue glass. Repeat this sequence three times. Add a silver spacer. Separate the wires.

String the Outer Strand:

1. On the outer strand, thread a 4mm blue glass bead.
2. Add on the outer strand a silver spacer, one 4mm tube, silver spacer, 6mm blue glass, silver spacer, four turquoise wheels, silver spacer, and 6mm blue glass. Repeat the sequence seven times.
3. Add a silver spacer, one 4mm tube, and 4mm blue glass. Clamp the end of the beaded strand while you bead the inner strand.

String the Inner Strand:

1. On the inner strand, thread a 4mm blue glass bead.
2. Add on the inner strand a silver spacer, one 4mm tube, silver spacer, 6mm blue glass, silver spacer, four turquoise wheels, silver spacer, and 6mm blue glass. Repeat the sequence six times.
3. Add a silver spacer, one 4mm tube bead, and 4mm blue glass. Bring wire ends together.

Finish:

1. On both wires, repeat the sequence from step 3 in the "Start" section in reverse. Add a 4mm blue glass bead to complete the other side of the necklace.
2. Add a crimp bead over both wire ends. Wrap the wires around other loop of the clasp, then back through crimp bead and several beads. Pull wires taut, but not tight - you want both necklace strands to dangle. Crimp bead. Cut wire tails.

EARRINGS

1. On one fancy head pin, thread a 6mm blue glass bead, silver spacer, five turquoise wheels, silver spacer, and 4mm blue glass bead.
2. Cut wire end 3/8" from last bead. Form a loop in wire end using roundnose pliers.
3. Attach ear wire loop to head pin loop.
4. Repeat steps 1 through 3 to make the other earring. ❏

GARNET SCALLOPS
necklace & earrings

The garnet beads used to make this necklace are reminiscent of the jewel-like seeds of the pomegranate. This necklace would be particularly effective when you wish to be creative or passionate.

Designed by Patty Cox

BEADING SUPPLIES

200 (approx.) round garnet beads, 4mm

24 flat-end diamond-shaped garnet beads

1 gold spring ring clasp

2 gold fish hook ear wires

Optional: 2 gold bead tips

Black beading thread

TOOLS & OTHER SUPPLIES

Beading needle

Scissors

INSTRUCTIONS

Necklace length: 17"

1. Thread a beading needle with 1-1/2 yards of black beading thread. Knot one thread end to one side of the clasp, leaving a 3" tail.
2. Thread three 4mm round beads and a diamond-shaped bead on the beading thread. Repeat this sequence 22 times, ending with three 4mm round beads. Knot thread on the other half of the clasp.
3. Pass the needle and thread back through three round beads and one diamond-shaped bead. Add five round beads on the thread, then thread the needle through the next diamond-shaped bead to make a beaded scallop. (Photo 1) Bring the thread back down and pick up five more beads. Continue adding scallops around the necklace until you reach the last diamond-shaped bead.
4. Pass the needle through the last three round beads. Knot the thread around the clasp. Run the thread tail back through several beads.
5. Thread the beginning 3" tail on the needle. Pass the thread tail back through several beads. Trim thread ends.
6. *Option:* Cover thread knots with bead tips.

EARRINGS

1. Thread a beading needle with 12" of black beading thread. Knot one thread end to an ear wire loop, leaving a 3" tail.
2. Thread a 4mm round bead, a diamond-shaped bead, and five 4mm round beads on the thread.
3. Pass the needle back through the diamond-shaped bead and first 4mm round bead. Knot thread on ear wire loop. Run the thread tails back through several beads. Trim thread end.
4. Repeat steps 1 through 3 to make the other earring. ❑

Photo 1 - Making the beaded scallops.

SEEING CLEARLY
labradorite glasses holder

Because labradorite is believed to help us gauge distance accurately and aid in detail work, it is the perfect stone for a glasses holder. Here, labradorite chip beads are combined with blue glass beads, abalone (for its rainbow colors), and hematite, which has a reputation for helping people bring order to mentally chaotic situations.

Designed by Patty Cox

BEADING SUPPLIES

150 (approx.) labradorite chip beads

Blue/green matte seed beads

5 abalone shell beads, 8x18mm

25 (approx.) faceted round gray hematite beads, 4mm

6 turquoise oval faceted glass beads, 8x12mm

20 silver beads, 3.2mm

Beading wire, .012

2-piece. eyeglasses holder

2 silver crimp beads

TOOLS & OTHER SUPPLIES

Wire cutters

Crimping tool

INSTRUCTIONS
Necklace length: 28"

1. Cut two 36" lengths of beading wire. Thread a crimp bead over both wire ends. Loop wires through one piece of the eyeglasses holder, then back through the crimp bead, leaving a 1-1/2" tail. Crimp bead.

2. Thread a 4mm hematite bead over both wires. Separate wires.

3. On one (the "first") wire, thread 1-1/8" of labradorite chip beads. On the other (the "second") wire, thread 12 seed beads. Thread the second wire through the center nugget on the first wire. Add 12 more seed beads on the second wire. (Photo 1)

4. Bring wire ends together. Thread a silver bead, hematite, turquoise oval, hematite and silver bead on both wires. (Photo 2) Separate wires.

5. Repeat step 3 one time.

6. Thread a silver bead, hematite, abalone shell bead, hematite, and silver bead. Separate wires.

7. Repeat step 3 one time.

8. Repeat steps 3 through 7 six times.

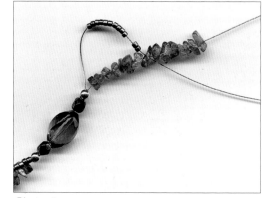
Photo 1

Photo 2

9. Thread a crimp bead over both wire ends. Loop wires through the other piece of the eyeglasses holder, then back through the crimp bead, leaving a 1-1/2" tail. Crimp bead. Cut wire tails.

10. To use, slide the loops of the eyeglasses holder over the earpieces of glasses next to the hinges. ❏

AMETHYST & PEACOCK BLUE
necklace & earrings

BEADING SUPPLIES

36 amethyst round beads, 6mm

7 amethyst round beads, 10mm

21 faceted peacock Czech glass beads, 4mm

26 faceted peacock Czech glass beads, 6mm

35 (approx.) amethyst glass beads, 4mm

40 (approx.) gold-plated beads, 2mm

60 (approx.) gold-plated beads, 3.2mm

26 gold filigree bead caps, 6mm

1 gold hook and eye clasp

4 gold crimp beads

2 gold ear wires

Beading wire, .012

TOOLS & OTHER SUPPLIES

Wire cutters

Crimping tool

Clamp *or* bead stopper

INSTRUCTIONS
Necklace length: 16"

Start:

1. Cut two 24" lengths of beading wire. Thread a crimp bead on both wires. Thread both wires around one side of the clasp, then back through the crimp bead. Crimp bead.
2. Thread a gold bead and a 4mm amethyst glass bead on both wire strands and wire tails. Separate strands.

String the Outer Strand:

1. On the outer wire, add a 2mm gold after each of the following beads in the sequence: 4mm peacock, 4mm amethyst, three 6mm amethyst, 4mm amethyst.
2. Continue stringing, add a 3.2mm gold. Then add a 3.2mm gold bead after each bead in the following sequence: 4mm peacock, 4mm amethyst, 6mm peacock, 6mm amethyst.
3. Add a bead cap, a 10mm amethyst, a bead cap.
4. Add a 3.2mm gold, then add a 3.2mm gold after each bead in the following sequence: 6mm amethyst, 6mm peacock, 4mm amethyst, 4mm peacock, 4mm amethyst, 6mm peacock, 6mm amethyst.
5. Add a bead cap, 10mm amethyst, bead cap.
6. Add a 3.2mm gold, then a 3.2mm bead after every bead in the following sequence: 6mm amethyst, 6mm peacock, 4mm amethyst, 4mm peacock, 4mm amethyst, 6mm peacock, 6mm amethyst.
7. Add a bead cap, 10mm amethyst, and bead cap.
8. Repeat steps 1-7 of this section in reverse to make the other half of the strand. Secure the end of the beaded strand with a stop bead or clamp while you string the inner strand.

String the Inner Strand:

1. On the inner strand, add a 3.2mm gold, 4mm peacock, 2mm gold, 4mm amethyst, 2mm gold, 6mm peacock, 3.2mm gold, 6mm amethyst, 3.2mm gold, bead cap, 6mm amethyst, bead cap, 3.2mm gold, 6mm amethyst, 3.2mm gold, 6mm peacock, 3.2mm gold, 4mm amethyst, 3.2mm gold, 4mm peacock, 3.2mm gold, 4mm amethyst, 3.2mm gold, 6mm peacock, 3.2mm gold, 6mm amethyst, 3.2mm gold, bead cap, 6mm amethyst, bead cap, 3.2mm gold, 6mm amethyst, 3.2mm gold, 6mm peacock, 3.2mm gold, 4mm amethyst, 3.2mm gold, 4mm peacock, 3.2mm gold, 4mm amethyst, 3.2mm gold, 6mm peacock, 3.2mm gold, 6mm amethyst, 3.2mm gold, bead cap, 10mm amethyst, bead cap, 3.2mm gold, 6mm amethyst, 3.2mm gold, 6mm peacock, 3.2mm gold, 4mm amethyst, and 3.2mm gold.
2. Add a 4mm peacock.
3. Repeat step 1 of this section in reverse to complete the inner strand.

Finish:

1. Bring both wire ends together. Thread a 4mm amethyst and 2mm gold bead on both strands. Thread a crimp bead on both wire ends.
2. Thread both wires around the other side of the clasp, then back through the crimp bead and several beads. Crimp bead. Cut wire tails.

EARRINGS

1. Cut two 8" lengths of beading wire.
2. On one wire, thread a 4mm peacock, 3.2mm gold, 6mm amethyst, 3.2mm gold, 4mm amethyst, 2mm gold, 4mm peacock, 2mm gold, 4mm amethyst, 3.2mm gold, 6mm peacock, 3.2mm gold, 6mm amethyst, 3.2mm gold, bead cap, 6mm amethyst, bead cap, 3.2mm gold, 6mm amethyst, 3.2mm gold, 6mm peacock, 3.2mm gold, 4mm amethyst, 2mm gold, 4mm peacock, 2mm gold, and 4mm amethyst.
3. Run the end of the wire back through the first three beads. Bring wire ends together. Thread a crimp bead over both wires.
4. Wrap the wires around one ear wire loop, then back through crimp bead and several beads. Pull wires taut, but not tight—allow the earring to dangle. Crimp bead. Cut wire tails.
5. Repeat steps 2 through 4 to make the other earring. ❑

In this necklace and earrings set, round amethyst beads in an array of sizes are combined with peacock blue glass beads and accented with gold. This healing stone will help to achieve tranquility and to alleviate negativity. Wear this necklace to calm the mind when you have had a day filled with a lot of mental activity.

Designed by Patty Cox

AMETHYST CLUSTER
pendant & earrings

This amethyst cluster pendant showcases the crystalline quality of amethyst, which is a variety of quartz. In this two-strand necklace, the gold setting of the pendant is complemented by sections of spiral-link gold chain. Wearing amethysts is believed to promote selflessness and to dispel rage, anger, fear, and anxiety.

Designed by Patty Cox

BEADING SUPPLIES

1 amethyst cluster pendant with bail, gold setting
132 amethyst matte beads, 4mm
60 (approx.) amethyst glass beads, 4mm
30 (approx.) gold plated beads, 3.2mm
12" gold chain with spiral links (You'll need 23 spiral links in all.)
1 gold hook-and-eye clasp
10 gold crimp beads
2 gold ear wires
2 gold head pins
2 gold eye pins
Beading wire, .012

TOOLS & OTHER SUPPLIES

Wire cutters
Crimping tool
Roundnose pliers
Ruler

INSTRUCTIONS
Necklace length: 21"

Cut the Chain:
1. Cut the spiral chain into three lengths with seven spiral links each. (Each section will be about 3-1/4" long.)
2. Set aside the remaining two spiral links for the earrings.

Start the Outer Strand:
In this section, you'll make the center part of the outer strand.
1. Cut a 12" length of beading wire. Thread a crimp bead on one end.
2. Wrap the wire end around one end of a gold chain section, then back through the crimp bead. Crimp bead.
3. Thread a gold bead, an amethyst glass, five amethyst matte beads, and an amethyst glass. Repeat two more times.
4. Add the amethyst cluster pendant to the wire.
5. Repeat step 3 in reverse.
6. Add a crimp bead. Thread the wire end around one end of another gold chain section, then back through the crimp bead. Pull the wire taut. Crimp bead.

Attach One Side of the Clasp:
In this section, you attach the clasp and complete one side of the outer strand.
1. Cut a 24" length and a 10" length of bead stringing wire. Thread a crimp bead over both wires. Thread the wire ends through one side of the clasp, then back through the crimp bead. Crimp bead.
2. On both wires, thread three amethyst matte beads and an amethyst glass bead. Separate wires.
3. On the short (10") wire, thread a gold bead, an amethyst glass, five amethyst matte beads, and an amethyst glass. Repeat two more times.
4. At the end of that wire, add a gold bead and a crimp bead.
5. Thread the wire end around one end of one gold chain section on the outer strand, which you made in the previous section, then back through the crimp bead. Pull wire taut. Crimp bead. (On the outer strand, you now have - in this order - a bead section, a

chain section, a longer bead section with the amethyst cluster pendant at the center of it, and a second gold chain section.)

Make the Inner Strand:
In this section, you'll make the inner strand, which has a chain section in the middle and beads on either end.
1. On the 24" wire, thread five amethyst matte beads and a gold glass bead.
2. Thread a gold bead, an amethyst glass, five amethyst matte beads, and an amethyst glass. Repeat five times.
3. At the end of that wire, add a gold bead and a crimp bead.
4. Thread the wire end around one end of the third gold chain section, then back through a crimp bead. Pull wire taut. Crimp bead. Cut wire end.
5. Attach the remaining piece of the 24" wire to the other end of the chain section with a crimp bead.
6. Add beads to match the other side of this strand. (Step 2 in reverse, step 1 in reverse). Secure the beads on the wire with a clamp or a stop bead.

Attach the Other Side of the Clasp:
In this section, you'll complete the final part of the outer strand and attach the other side of the clasp.
1. Cut a 10" length of bead stringing wire.
2. Thread the wire end around one end of the third gold chain section, then back through a crimp bead. Pull wire taut. Crimp bead. Cut wire end.

continued on page 98

continued from page 96

3. Thread beads on the wire to match the other end of the outer strand, finishing with a gold bead.
4. Remove the clamp or stop bead from the inner strand. Bring both wires together.
5. Thread both wires through the last five beads: an amethyst glass, three amethyst matte bead, and a gold seed bead. Add a crimp bead.
6. Thread both wires through the other side of the clasp, then back through the crimp bead and last five beads.

Pull wires taut. Crimp bead. Cut wire ends.

EARRINGS

1. On a head pin, thread a gold bead, an amethyst glass bead, three amethyst matte beads, an amethyst glass bead, and a gold bead.
2. Trim the head pin wire end to 3/8". Make a loop in the wire end with roundnose pliers.
3. Attach the loop to one end of one the reserved spiral chain links.

4. On an eye pin, thread a gold bead, an amethyst glass bead, three amethyst matte beads, an amethyst glass bead, and a gold bead.
5. Trim the eye pin wire end to 3/8". Make a loop in the wire end with roundnose pliers.
6. Attach the loop to an ear wire. Attach the other loop of the eye pin to the spiral chain link.
7. Repeat steps 1 through six to make the other earring. ❑

GIFTS FROM THE SEA
shell pendant & earrings

Two gifts from the sea - coral and mother of pearl - bring peaceful healing energy that can quiet the emotions and aid visualization. The salmon color of the coral and the warm luminescence of the mother of pearl are linked in the coloration of the shell pendant, another gift from the sea. In Buddhist worship, the conch shell is a symbol of the spoken word.

Designed by Patty Cox

BEADING SUPPLIES

50 (approx.) salmon bamboo coral rice beads, 4x6mm
52 mother of pearl round beads, 5mm
52 mother of pearl round beads, 6mm
1 transverse spiral shell pendant
1 silver jump ring, 7mm
1 silver crimp bead
2 silver ear wires
Beading wire, .012

TOOLS & OTHER SUPPLIES

Wire cutters
Crimping tool

INSTRUCTIONS

Necklace length: 25"

Pendant

1. Thread a 7mm silver jump ring in the top hole of the shell pendant. Close the ring.
2. Cut 1 yd. bead stringing wire.
3. Thread beads on the wire: a 4x6mm salmon coral rice bead, 6mm mother of pearl, 5mm mother of pearl, 4x6mm salmon coral rice bead, 5mm mother of pearl, 6mm mother of pearl, 4x6mm salmon coral rice bead.
4. Add in this order: a 6mm mother of pearl, 5mm mother of pearl, 4x6mm salmon coral rice bead, 5mm mother of pearl, 6mm mother of pearl, 4x6mm salmon coral rice bead. Repeat nine times.
5. Add a 6mm mother of pearl, 5mm mother of pearl, shell pendant, 5mm mother of pearl.
6. Repeat the sequence in step 4 ten times, ending with a crimp bead.
7. Thread the beginning wire through a crimp bead and several adjacent

beads. Thread ending wire through several beads. Pull wires taut. Crimp bead. Cut wire tails.

EARRINGS

1. Cut two 10" lengths of bead stringing wire.
2. On one wire, thread a 6mm mother of pearl, 5mm mother of pearl, 4x6mm salmon coral rice bead, 5mm mother of pearl, 6mm mother of pearl, 4x6mm salmon coral rice bead. Repeat three times, leaving off the last salmon coral rice bead on the final repeat.
3. Add a crimp bead and an ear wire. Thread the beginning wire through the crimp bead, ear wire, and several adjacent beads. Thread ending wire through several beads. Pull wires taut. Crimp bead. Cut wire tails.
4. Repeat steps 2 and 3 to make the other earring. ❑

BALTIC ELEGANCE
amber choker & earrings

Wear this set to transform negative energy to positive.
Amber can help improve your luck, strength and love life.

Designed by Patty Cox

BEADING SUPPLIES

28 Baltic amber oval beads, 8x12mm
Mahogany seed beads
21 bronze faceted Czech glass beads, 4mm
16 bronze faceted Czech glass beads, 6mm
24 fluted 24-kt. gold-plated beads, 4mm
12 fluted 24-kt. gold-plated beads, 5mm
22 fluted 24-kt. gold-plated beads, 6mm
1 gold-filled filigree clasp
2 gold fish hook ear wires
2 gold head pins
2 gold crimp beads
Beading wire, .015

TOOLS & OTHER SUPPLIES

Wire cutters
Crimping tool
Roundnose pliers
Ruler

INSTRUCTIONS

Necklace length: 15"

Make the Head Pin Dangles:

1. Thread beads on head pins according to Fig. A, making 23 beaded head pin dangles in all.
2. Cut each head pin wire 3/8" from the last bead. Form a loop in the wire end, using roundnose pliers.

Assemble the Necklace:

1. Cut a 24" length of beading wire. Thread a crimp bead on the wire end. Thread the wire end through one side of the clasp, then back through the crimp bead, leaving a 1" tail. Crimp bead.
2. To make one side of the necklace, begin with a seed bead, twelve 4mm gold beads, six 5mm gold beads. Add a seed bead between each of the gold beads. Thread the first beads on the wire and over the wire tail.
3. To make the front part of the necklace, add a seed bead, a head pin side dangle, and a 6mm gold bead. Continue adding seed beads, head pin dangles, 6mm gold beads to complete the front of the necklace. See the Legend for Fig. A regarding the placement of the dangles.
4. Finish the other side of the necklace, adding six 5mm gold beads, then twelve 4mm gold beads with a seed bead between each gold bead.
5. Add a gold crimp bead on the end of the wire. Thread wire end through the other side of the clasp, then back through the crimp bead and several beads. Pull wire taut. Crimp bead. Cut wire tail.

EARRINGS

1. On a head pin, thread a seed bead, 6mm faceted, seed bead, amber bead, seed bead, 4mm faceted, and seed bead.
2. Cut the head pin wire 3/8" from the last bead. Form a loop in the wire end with roundnose pliers.
3. Open the loop of an ear wire and attach to head pin loop.
4. Repeat steps 1 through 3 to make the other earring. ❏

Fig. A - The Beaded Dangles

#1 - Make 8 and put 4 on each side of the center dangle. Sequence: Seed bead, 4mm faceted, seed bead, amber, seed bead.

#2 - Make 8 and put 4 on each side of the center dangle. Sequence: Seed bead, 6mm faceted, seed bead, amber, seed bead.

#3 - Make 2 and put 1 on each side of the center dangle. Sequence: Seed bead, 4mm faceted, seed bead, amber, seed bead, 4mm faceted.

#4 - Make 2 and put 1 on each side of the center dangle. Sequence: Seed bead, 6mm faceted, seed bead, amber, seed bead, 4mm faceted, seed bead.

#5 - Make 2 and put 1 on each side of the center dangle. Sequence: Seed bead, 4mm faceted, seed bead, amber, seed bead, 6mm faceted, seed bead, amber, seed bead, 4 mm faceted, seed bead.

#6 (Center) - Make 1. Sequence: Seed bead, 6mm faceted, seed bead, amber, seed bead, 4mm faceted, seed bead, amber, seed bead, 6mm faceted, seed bead.

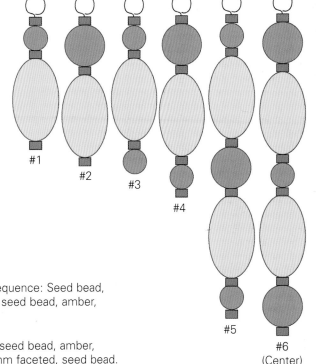

TRANSFORMATION
obsidian necklace & earrings

Snowflake obsidian rondells and a disc are combined with onyx beads and sections of silver chain. This necklace has transforming powers because of the use of obsidian, which can help overcome obsessions, and onyx - a stone that protects against negative forces. Also, a symbol of transformation, a silver butterfly charm is suspended from the disc.

Designed by Patty Cox

BEADING SUPPLIES

100 (approx.) snowflake obsidian rondelles, 6mm

1 snowflake obsidian disc, 35mm

9 round black onyx beads, 8mm

14 round black onyx beads, 3mm

13 pieces silver-plated 2.3mm figaro chain, 2" long

1 silver-plated lobster clasp

2 silver head pins

2 silver eye pins

2 silver ear wires

40 (approx.) silver jump rings, 4mm

1 silver butterfly charm

2 silver crimp beads

Beading wire, .015

TOOLS & OTHER SUPPLIES

Wire cutters

Crimping tool

Roundnose pliers

Ruler

INSTRUCTIONS
Necklace length: 26"

Make the Beaded Eye Pins:
1. On an eye pin, thread two snowflake obsidian rondelles, an 8mm onyx bead, and two snowflake obsidian rondelles. Cut wire 3/8" from the last bead. Form a loop in the wire end using roundnose pliers. Repeat the process to make six in all.
2. On an eye pin, thread a 3mm black onyx bead, five snowflake obsidian rondelles, and a 3mm black onyx bead. Cut wire 3/8" from the last bead. Form a loop in the wire end using roundnose pliers. Repeat the process to make four in all.

Make the Center of the Outer Strand:
1. Wrap a 2" length of chain through the disc. Secure snugly against the disc with a jump ring, allowing the end of the chain to fall below the disc.
2. Attach the butterfly charm to the end of the chain with a jump ring.
3. Wrap a 2" length of chain through the top of the disc to make a loop for hanging. Secure the chain snugly around the disc with a jump ring. Cut excess chain from around the jump ring.
4. Attach the jump ring on the hanging loop to the center of a 2" chain length to make the necklace center.

Make the Center of the Inner Strand:
1. Cut a 10" length of bead stringing wire. Thread a crimp bead on one wire end. Run the wire end back through the crimp bead, forming a 1/8" loop. Crimp bead.
2. Thread 19 snowflake obsidian rondelle beads on the wire. Add an 8mm black onyx bead and 19 snowflake obsidian rondelle beads.
3. Thread a crimp bead on the wire end. Thread the wire tail back through the crimp bead and several rondelle beads. Pull wires taut. Crimp bead. Cut wire tail.

Assemble Outer Strand:
1. Attach one of the beaded eye pins to 12" chain piece with a jump ring. You'll have ten in all - six for the outer strand and four for the inner strand. Set aside four of these.
2. On each end of the outer strand center 2" chain, working from the center to the end, attach in this order: an beaded eye pin with 8mm onyx + 2" chain, a beaded eye pin with 5 rondelles + 2" chain, a beaded eye pin with 8mm onyx + a 2" chain, using jump rings.

Assemble Inner Strand & Finish:
1. On each end of the inner strand center, attach a 2" chain + beaded eye pin with 8mm onyx and a 2" chain + a beaded eye pin with 5 rondelles.

2. Bring the necklace strands together on each side. Attach one end of each strand to one side of the clasp with a jump ring.

3. Attach the remaining ends to the other side of the clasp with a jump ring.

EARRINGS

1. On a head pin, thread a 3mm black onyx, a snowflake obsidian rondelle, and an 8mm black onyx. Cut wire 3/8" from last bead. Form a loop in the wire end using roundnose pliers. Make two beaded head pins.

2. On an eye pin, thread a 3mm black onyx, five snowflake obsidian rondelles, and a 3mm black onyx. Cut the wire 3/8" from the last bead. Form a loop in the wire end using roundnose pliers. Make two beaded eye pins.

3. Connect one beaded eye pin to a 1/2" piece of silver chain with a jump ring.

4. Attach the beaded head pin to the other end of the chain piece with a jump ring.

5. Attach the top loop of the eye pin to an ear wire loop.

6. Repeat steps 3, 4, and 5 to make the second earring, using the remaining beaded head pin and eye pin. ❏

PROSPERITY & ABUNDANCE
jade & coins set

Jade is thought to encourage wisdom, courage, and clarity and to be the stone of health, wealth, and long life. Long prized in China, jade beads are combined in this necklace with Chinese coins in two sizes and glass and metal beads.

Designed by Patty Cox

BEADING SUPPLIES

20 jade beads, 8mm

Green Czech glass bead mix

Lime transparent seed beads, size 6/0

20 (approx.) antique silver beads, 5mm

20 (approx.) antique gold bead caps, 8mm

20 (approx.) filigree bead caps, 9mm

20 (approx.) antique gold spacer beads, 6mm

26 antique gold disc spacers, 6mm

20 antique gold bicone spacer beads

8 Chinese coins with loops, 15mm

8 Chinese coins with loops, 20mm

16 bronze jump rings, 5mm

15 bronze head pins, 2"

2 bronze eye pins

1 bronze toggle clasp

2 bronze ear wires

2 crimp beads

Beading wire, .018

TOOLS & OTHER SUPPLIES

Needlenose pliers

Roundnose pliers

Crimping tool

INSTRUCTIONS
Necklace length: 19"

Make the Beaded & Coin Dangles:

1. On a head pin, thread:
   - a 5mm antique silver bead *or a* 4mm glass bead
   - a bead cap
   - an 8mm jade bead *or a* glass bead (8mm to 12mm)
   - a bead cap
   - a 6mm glass bead
   - a 5mm antique silver bead *or a* small glass bead and a spacer bead.

The beaded dangles will vary slightly, depending on the beads you select. See Photo 1.

2. Cut the head pin wire 3/8" from the last bead. Form the wire into a loop using roundnose pliers (Photo 1).

3. Install a jump ring in the top loop of each 20mm coin and six of the 15mm coins. Reserve the two remaining 15mm coins for the earrings.

String the Beads:

1. Cut 26" of bead stringing wire. To make the center drop, thread a 5mm antique silver bead, 8mm jade, glass disc spacer, bicone spacer, glass disc spacer, 5mm antique silver bead, bead cap, 12mm glass bead, bead cap, 5mm antique silver beads, and a seed bead. Bring beads to wire center. Loop one wire end around the seed bead, then back through all the beads. Gently pull the wire, bringing the beads loosely together. (Photo 2) Separate the wires.

2. On one wire, thread a 6mm gold disc spacer, lime seed, 20mm coin, lime seed, bicone spacer, lime seed, head pin dangle, lime seed, gold disc spacer, 8mm jade bead, and gold disc spacer. Repeat the sequence six times. On the first three repeats, use 20mm coins. On the last three repeats, use 15mm coins.

3. Add a lime seed, bicone spacer, lime seed, head pin dangle, lime seed, bicone spacer, lime seed, 5mm antique silver bead, and a crimp bead. Thread wire end around one side of the clasp, then back through the crimp bead and several beads. Pull wire taut. Crimp bead. Cut wire tail.

4. Repeat steps 2 and 3 to make the other side of the necklace.

EARRINGS

1. On an eye pin, thread a 5mm antique silver bead, bead cap, 8mm jade bead, bead cap, a glass bead (4mm to 6mm), and 5mm antique silver bead.

2. Cut the eye pin wire 3/8" from the last bead. Form the wire end into a loop, using roundnose pliers.

3. Attach the top loop of the eye pin to an ear wire loop. Attach bottom eye pin loop to the loop on a small coin.

4. Repeat steps 1 through 3 to make the other earring. ❑

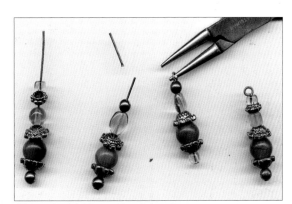

Photo 1 - Making a bead dangle.

Photo 2 - Stringing the center drop.

PINK LADDER
rose quartz bracelet

BEADING SUPPLIES

24 rose quartz tubes, 4x13mm

46 pink matte Czech glass beads, size 6/0

Silver-lined clear seed beads

1 silver lobster clasp, 12mm

1 silver crimp bead

Beading wire, .012

TOOLS & OTHER SUPPLIES

Wire cutters

Crimping tool

INSTRUCTIONS

Bracelet length: 8"

1. Cut 1-1/4 yards of beading wire. Thread one side of the lobster clasp on the wire. Center the clasp piece on the wire (Photo 1).
2. Bring wire ends together. thread a clear seed bead on both wires. Push the seed bead next to the clasp piece (Photo 2).
3. Separate the wires. Thread six clear seed beads on each wire. (Photo 3).
4. On the left wire, thread a clear seed bead, 6/0 pink matte, and two clear seed beads
5. Add a rose quartz tube bead to the left wire.
6. On the right wire, add the same bead sequence in step 4.
7. Thread the right wire through the rose quartz tube bead. Thread each wire through a clear seed bead on each end of tube (Photo 4).
8. Repeat steps 4, 5, 6, and 7 until the bracelet is about 6-1/2" long (or your desired length).
9. Add six clear seed beads on each wire. Bring wire ends together. Add a clear seed bead and a crimp bead.
10. Thread the other side of the clasp on both wires. Bring wires around clasp and back through the crimp bead. Thread each wire end back through five seed beads. Pull wires taut. Crimp bead. Cut wire ends close to seed beads. ❑

Photo 1 - Center the clasp piece on the wire.

Photo 2 - Thread a clear seed bead next to the clasp.

Photo 3 - Separate wires and add beads.

Photo 4 - Thread each wire end through a seed bead at each end of the rose quartz tube bead.

Beautiful rose quartz beads used to make this bracelet form a ladder or bridge toward positive change. Wearing it can remind us that change is important, even difficult change, and can help us be more open to other people.

Designed by Patty Cox

ROSE QUARTZ SPARKLE
necklace & earrings

Known as the love stone, rose quartz is also used to assist with problems of the heart. It is believed to bring peacefulness and calm to relationships, and to inspire forgiveness and hasten self-acceptance. Here, the rosy color is enhanced with the sparkle of pink rhinestones and the glow of glass pearls.

Designed by Patty Cox

BEADING SUPPLIES

11 rose quartz round beads, 8mm

5 rose quartz round beads, 6mm

3 rhinestone ball beads, 10mm

22 rhinestone rondelle wheels, 6mm

120 (approx.) white glass pearls, 5mm

1 pearl drop, 30mm

2 silver toggle clasps (The loop of the second clasp is used for attaching the drop.)

4 silver spacer beads, 6mm

2 silver spacer beads, 4mm

4 silver crimp beads

4 silver head pins

1 silver jump ring

2 sterling silver ear posts with split loops

Beading wire, .012

TOOLS & OTHER SUPPLIES

Wire cutters

Roundnose pliers

Crimping tool

INSTRUCTIONS
Necklace length: 25"

String the Beads:

1. Cut 1 yd. of beading wire. Thread a crimp bead on one end. Run the wire through one side of the toggle clasp, then back through the crimp bead, leaving a 2" tail. Crimp the bead.
2. Thread beads on wire in this order: a 4mm silver spacer bead, seven pearls, 6mm silver spacer bead, 22 pearls, 6mm silver spacer bead, seven pearls, rhinestone wheel, 8mm rose quartz, rhinestone wheel, white pearl, 6mm rose quartz, white pearl, rhinestone wheel, 8mm rose quartz, rhinestone wheel, three white pearls, 10mm rhinestone ball bead, three pearls, rhinestone wheel, 8mm rose quartz, rhinestone wheel, pearl, 6mm rose quartz, pearl, rhinestone wheel, 8mm rose quartz, rhinestone wheel, and three white pearls.
3. Add a 10mm rhinestone ball bead.
4. Repeat step 2 in reverse to make the other half of the necklace.
5. Add a crimp bead on the end of the wire. Thread the end of the wire through the other side of the toggle clasp, then back through crimp bead and several beads. Crimp. Cut wire tail.

Add the Center Dangle:
See Photo 1.

1. On the center rhinestone ball bead, thread a head pin through the top of the bead. (Rhinestone ball beads have spaces between the rhinestones.)
2. Cut the wire end of the head pin 3/8" from the ball bead. Form wire end into a loop, using roundnose pliers.

Attach the loop of the second toggle clasp to the loop on the head pin with a jump ring.

3. Thread a head pin through the pearl drop. Cut the wire end of the head pin 3/8" from the bead. Form a loop in the wire end, using roundnose pliers.
4. Cut 8" of beading wire. Thread a crimp bead on wire. Thread one end of the wire around the toggle loop, then back through the crimp bead, leaving a 1" tail. Crimp.
5. Thread these beads on the wire and over the wire tail: seven pearls, rhinestone wheel, 8mm rose quartz, rhinestone wheel, pearl, and 6mm rose quartz, pearl. Add a crimp bead.
6. Run the wire through the loop of the pearl drop, then back through the crimp bead and several beads. Gently pull wire to bring dangle beads together. Crimp. Cut wire tail.

EARRINGS

1. On a head pin, thread a pearl, rhinestone wheel, 8mm rose quartz, rhinestone wheel, and pearl.
2. Cut the head pin wire end 3/8" from the last bead. Form a loop in the wire end, using roundnose pliers.
3. Attach the loop to an ear post with a jump ring.
4. Repeat steps 1, 2, and 3 to make the other earring. ❏

Photo 1 - Threading a head pin through a rhinestone ball bead, **left**, and making a loop in the end of the wire with roundnose pliers, **right**.

GOLDEN TONES
tiger's eye & amber set

The warm tones of tiger's eye and amber are believed to bring healing earth energy and glowing warmth to the wearer. Tiger's eye is a good stone for people who need more confidence to accomplish their goals; amber aids in making correct choices.

Designed by Patty Cox

BEADING SUPPLIES

28 tiger's eye rectangle beads, 9x14mm
20 round tiger's eye beads, 6mm
12 Baltic amber beads, 8x12mm
60 (approx.) 24-kt. gold-plated beads, 2.4mm
36 24-kt. gold-plated spacer beads, 5mm
8" gold chain
6 gold crimp beads
1 gold 3-into-1 connector
1 gold spring ring clasp
2 gold ear wires
4 gold jump rings
2 gold head pins, 2"
Beading wire, .012

TOOLS & OTHER SUPPLIES

Wire cutters
Crimping tool

INSTRUCTIONS

Necklace length: 18"

Make the Inner (9") Strand:

1. Cut 14" of beading wire. Thread a crimp bead on the end of the wire. Thread the wire end through an outer hole of the 3-into-1 connector, then back through the crimp bead, leaving a 1" tail. Crimp bead.
2. Add these beads on the wire and over the wire tail: 2.4mm gold, tiger's eye rectangle, and 2.4mm gold.
3. Add a 5mm gold, 2.4mm gold, 6mm tiger's eye round, 2.4mm gold, 5mm gold, 2.4mm gold, tiger's eye rectangle, and 2.4mm gold. Repeat this sequence five more times.
4. End the strand with a crimp bead.
5. Thread the wire end through an outer hole of the other end of the 3-into-1 connector, then back through the crimp bead and several beads. Pull wire taut, but not tight - allow the strand to dangle. Crimp bead. Cut wire end.

Make the Middle (10-1/2") Strand:

1. Cut 16" of bead stringing wire. Thread a crimp bead on the end of the wire. Thread the wire end through the center hole of the 3-into-1 connector, then back through crimp bead, leaving a 1" tail. Crimp bead.
2. Add these beads on the wire and over the wire tail: 2.4mm gold, amber, 2.4mm gold, tiger eye rectangle. Repeat this sequence eight times.
3. End the strand with a 2.4mm gold, an amber, a 2.4mm gold, and a crimp bead.
4. Thread the wire end through the center hole of the other end of the 3-into-1 connector, then back through the crimp bead and several beads. Pull wire taut, but not tight - allow the strand to dangle. Crimp bead. Cut wire end.

Make the Outer (11-1/2") Strand:

1. Cut 18" of bead stringing wire. Thread a crimp bead on the end of the wire. Thread the wire end through the remaining outer hole of the 3-into-1 connector, then back through the crimp bead, leaving a 1" tail. Crimp bead.
2. Add a 2.4mm gold bead on the wire and over the wire tail.
3. Then add these beads: 5mm gold, 6mm tiger eye, 5mm gold, tiger eye rectangle. Repeat this sequence nine times.
4. End the strand with a 5mm gold, 6mm tiger eye, 5mm gold, 2.4mm gold, and a crimp bead.
5. Thread the wire end through the remaining outer hole of the other 3-into-1 connector, then back through crimp bead and several beads. Pull wire taut, but not tight - allow the strand to dangle. Crimp bead. Cut wire end.

Add the Chain & Clasp:

1. Attach 4" of gold chain to one 3-into-1 connector with a jump ring.
2. Attach one side of the clasp to the end of the chain with a jump ring.
3. Repeat steps 1 and 2 to complete the other side of the necklace.

EARRINGS

1. On a head pin, thread a 2.4mm gold bead, 6mm tiger eye, 2.4mm gold, amber, 2.4mm gold, tiger eye rectangle, 2.4mm gold, 5mm gold, and 2.4mm gold.
2. Form the end of the head pin into a loop, using roundnose pliers.
3. Open the loop on an ear wire and attach to the loop at the top of the head pin.
4. Repeat steps 1 through 3 to make the other earring. ❏

HEART & SOUL
aventurine rosary

Use this rosary as a meditation and spiritual tool. The use of aventurine
in the design will help bring about inner peace and heal the heart by
releasing emotional stress and reuniting the heart and soul.

Designed by Patty Cox

BEADING SUPPLIES

53 round light aventurine beads, 6mm (Aves)
12 round sterling silver-plated beads, 2.4mm
6 silver filigree round spacer beads, 6mm (Paters)
Teal matte seed beads
1 silver Madonna 3-point connector
1 silver cross, 28mm
4 silver crimp beads
Beading wire, .012

TOOLS & OTHER SUPPLIES

Wire cutters
Crimping tool

About the Rosary

A rosary is a sacramental devotional aid used by
Roman Catholics. A rosary is used to combine
prayer and meditation. When using a rosary, a set
number of prayers is recited, and a string of beads
is used to keep count or the prayers. A rosary
usually is made up of five sets of "decades" of ten
beads for the recitation of the "Hail, Mary"
separated by a single bead for the recitation of the
Lord's Prayer. The name of the rosary comes from
the Latin *rosarium,* "crown of roses."

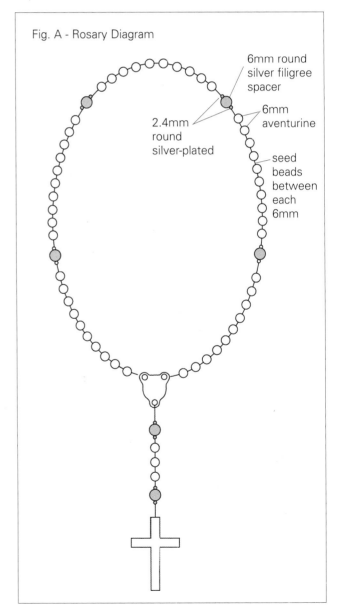

Fig. A - Rosary Diagram

6mm round
silver filigree
spacer

2.4mm
round
silver-plated

6mm
aventurine

seed
beads
between
each
6mm

INSTRUCTIONS

1. Cut 1 yd. of beading wire. Thread a crimp bead on the wire. Thread the end of the wire through one of the side holes in the 3-point connector, then back through the crimp bead, leaving a 1" tail. Crimp bead.

2. Thread seven seed beads on both wires (the wire and the wire tail).

3. Add a 6mm aventurine bead and three seed beads. Repeat nine times to complete the first decade or series of ten beads (Aves).

4. Add a 2.4mm silver bead, a 6mm silver bead (Pater), and a 2.4mm silver bead.

5. Repeat to complete five decades (step 3) with four Pater sections (step 4) between them. See Fig. A.

6. End with seven seed beads and a crimp bead. Thread the wire through other side hole in the op of the 3-point connector, then back through the crimp bead and several beads. Pull wire taut. Crimp bead. Cut wire tail.

7. Use the remaining bead stringing wire to make the pendant. Thread a crimp bead on the wire. Thread the end of the wire through the bottom hole in the 3-point connector, then back through the crimp bead, leaving a 1" tail. Crimp bead.

8. Thread seven seed beads, 2.4mm silver, 6mm silver, 2.4mm silver, three seed beads, 6mm aventurine, three seed beads, 6mm aventurine, three seed beads, 6mm aventurine, three seed beads, 2.4mm silver, 6mm silver, 2.4mm silver, seven seed beads, and a crimp bead.

9. Thread the wire through the top of the cross, then back through the crimp bead and several beads. Pull wire taut. Crimp bead. Cut wire tail. ❏

INVITATION TO SPIRIT
turquoise anglican prayer beads

Turquoise has a long history as a spiritual stone that enhances peace of
mind, wisdom, strength, and positive thinking. It is believed to open lines
of communication and to open the heart for giving and receiving.

Designed by Patty Cox

BEADING SUPPLIES

28 round turquoise beads, 8mm

1 turquoise round bead, 10mm
(invitatory bead)

4 silver rose beads, 9mm

48 turquoise matte glass beads, 4mm

1 pewter cross pendant, 23x33mm

1 silver crimp bead

Beading wire, .015

TOOLS &
OTHER SUPPLIES

Wire cutters

Crimping tool

Clamp *or* bead stopper

INSTRUCTIONS

See Photo 1.

1. Cut 24" of bead stringing wire. Add a stop bead or clamp at wire end.
2. Thread three 4mm beads on the wire.
3. Alternate an 8mm bead and a 4mm bead seven times (completing one week).
4. Add a 4mm bead, 9mm rose bead (cruciform bead), and two 4mm beads.
5. Repeat step 3, then step 4, then step 3, then step 4, and then step 3. (You will have four groups of seven beads and three cruciform rose beads.)
6. Finish the single strand beading with three 4mm beads.
7. Bring both wire ends together. Thread a 4mm bead on both strands. Add a rose bead, three 4mm beads, the 10mm invitatory bead, three 4mm beads, and a crimp bead.
8. Thread both wires through the hanging loop of the cross pendant, then back through the crimp bead and several beads. Pull wires taut. Crimp. Cut wire tails. ❏

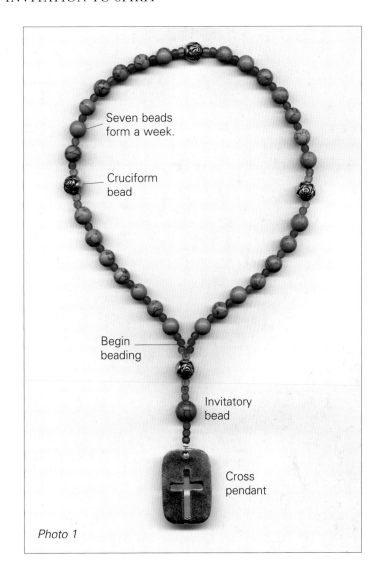

Seven beads
form a week.

Cruciform
bead

Begin
beading

Invitatory
bead

Cross
pendant

Photo 1

JOYOUS JASPER
choker & earrings

Jasper is believed to protect us from negativity and reduce our fears. In this necklace-and-earring set, jasper beads of many colors are combined with gold pearls and gold bead accents.

Designed by Patty Cox

BEADING SUPPLIES

41 round fancy jasper beads, 8mm

26 gold glass pearls, 6mm

7 gold glass pearls, 10mm

20, 24-kt. gold-plated round beads, 4mm

4, 24-kt. gold-plated round beads, 2.4mm

30 gold spacer beads, 6mm

4 fancy gold bead caps, 8mm

10 gold filigree bead caps, 6mm

1 gold jump ring

1 gold hook-and-eye clasp

2 gold crimp beads

2 gold fancy head pins

2 gold ear wires

Beading wire, .014

Optional: Gold chain with dangle, 3"

TOOLS & OTHER SUPPLIES

Wire cutters

Crimping tool

Clamp *or* stop bead

INSTRUCTIONS
Necklace length: 15"

Choker
Start:
1. Cut two 20" lengths of beading wire. Thread a crimp bead on both wires. Thread the wires through one side of the clasp, then back through the crimp bead, leaving 1" tails.
2. Thread a 4mm gold bead and 6mm pearl over both wires and tails. Repeat three more times, ending with a 4mm gold bead. Separate the wires.

Make the Outer Strand:
1. Thread beads in this order: 2.4mm gold, 4mm gold, 6mm pearl, spacer, three jasper beads, spacer, 6mm pearl, spacer, two 8mm jasper beads, spacer, 6mm pearl, spacer, three 8mm jasper beads, spacer, 10mm pearl, spacer, 8mm jasper bead, spacer, 10mm pearl, fancy bead cap, 8mm jasper, fancy bead cap.
2. Add the center 10mm pearl to the center.
3. Repeat step 1 in reverse to make the other half of the outer strand. Clamp the end of the wire while you string the inner strand.

Inner Strand:
1. Thread beads in this order: 2.4mm gold, 4mm gold, 6mm pearl, 4mm gold, 8mm jasper, 4mm gold, 6mm pearl, spacer, two 8mm jasper, spacer, 6mm pearl, spacer, three 8mm jasper beads, spacer, 6mm pearl, spacer, two 8mm jasper beads, spacer, 6mm pearl, spacer, 8mm jasper, and 8mm bead cap.
2. Add an 8mm jasper bead.
3. Repeat step 1 in reverse to make the other half of the inner strand.

Finish:
1. Bring the ends of the wires together. Thread a 4mm gold bead and a 6mm pearl over both wires. Repeat three times. Add a 4mm gold bead and a crimp bead.
2. Thread both wires through the other side of the clasp, then back through the crimp bead and several beads. Pull wires taut. Crimp bead. Cut wire tails.
3. *Option:* Add a 3" gold chain with a dangle to the loop side of the clasp.

EARRINGS
1. On a fancy head pin, thread a bead cap, 10mm pearl, bead cap, 8mm jasper, bead cap, 6mm pearl, bead cap, and 4mm gold.
2. Cut the head pin wire 3/8" from the last bead. Form wire into a loop, using roundnose pliers.
3. Attach the loop on an ear wire to the head pin loop.
4. Repeat steps 1 through 3 to make the other earring. ❏

PERIDOT & FAIRY
pendant necklace & earrings

Peridot, which is found in meteorites, is believed to be a good luck stone. Said to bring understanding of purpose, it aids in transforming physical work into material abundance. In this necklace, peridot chips are combined with green glass leaf beads and liquid silver beads and accented with a pewter fairy.

Designed by Patty Cox

BEADING SUPPLIES

28" strand of peridot bead chips

Liquid silver beads, 1.5x6mm

12 green glass leaf beads

1 pewter fairy with crystal pendant

Lime seed beads, 6/0 (E beads)

1 heart toggle clasp

2 silver ear wires

2 silver crimp beads

Beading wire, .014

TOOLS & OTHER SUPPLIES

Wire cutters

Crimping tool

INSTRUCTIONS

Necklace length: 22"

Start:

1. Cut two 28" lengths of beading wire. Thread a crimp bead on both wires. Thread wires through one side of the toggle clasp, then back through the crimp bead, leaving 1" tails.

2. Thread a liquid silver bead over both wires and tails. Separate the wires.

String the Beads:

1. On each wire, thread 1" of peridot bead chips. Bring wire ends together.

2. Thread a liquid silver bead, leaf bead and another liquid silver bead on both wires. Separate wires.

3. Thread 1" of peridot bead chips on each wire. Bring wire ends together.

4. Repeat steps 2 and 3 four times. Separate wires. Add a 1" length peridot bead chips on each wire. Bring wire ends together. Thread a liquid silver bead on both wires.

5. On the lower wire, thread three green 6/0 round beads. Bring the wire through the pendant loop, then back through the three green 6/0 beads. Bring both wire ends together. Thread a liquid silver bead on both wires.

6. String the beads for the second half of the necklace, which is a mirror image of the first half.

7. Bring the ends of the wires together. Thread a liquid silver bead and a crimp bead on both wires. Thread the wires through the other side of the toggle clasp, then back through the crimp bead and liquid silver bead. Pull wires taut. Crimp bead. Cut wire tails.

EARRINGS

1. Cut two 6" lengths of bead stringing wire.

2. Thread 1" of peridot bead chips on one wire. Add a liquid silver bead, a leaf bead, and a liquid silver bead. Thread another 1" of peridot bead chips on the wire.

3. Bring the two wire ends together and thread a green 6/0 bead and a crimp bead on both wires. Thread wires through an ear wire loop, then back through the crimp bead and 6/0 bead. Pull wires taut. Crimp bead. Cut wire tails.

4. Repeat steps 2 and 3 to make the other earring, using the other piece of wire. ❏

pearls were used to create this mala, which is embellished with two fish, which are Buddhist symbols representing spiritual liberation. Malas are used by Buddhists to count prayers or mantras.

Designed by Patty Cox

BEADING SUPPLIES

27 aqua pearls, 8mm

3 round coral beads, 5mm

2 gold beads, 3mm

2 cloisonne-enameled articulating fish pendants

Stretch nylon cording, 5mm

TOOLS & OTHER SUPPLIES

Scissors

Beading glue

Crimping tool

INSTRUCTIONS

See Fig. A.

1. Cut 14" of stretch nylon cording. Thread nine aqua pearls on the cording. Add a coral bead, nine aqua pearls, a coral bead, and nine aqua pearls.

2. Bring the ends of the cording together. Thread both ends through a gold bead, a coral bead, and a gold bead. Add a crimp bead on both ends. Separate the two pieces.

3. Add a fish pendant on one piece, then bring it back through the crimp bead and a gold bead. Repeat the process for the other piece of cording to attach the other fish pendant.

4. Tightly knot the cording together in a square knot. Dot knot with glue. Crimp bead.

5. Bring both ends of the cording up through another bead or two. Tightly knot the cording in a square knot. Dot knot with glue. When the is dry, cut the tails. ❑

About Malas

Malas are prayer beads that help keep your mind spiritually focused. Malas have been tradition and sacred spiritual tools of the Buddist and Hindu religions. The strings of beads are worn over the hand or in the hand so that each bead can be counted as each prayer is recited. Malas can include pendants of Buddist symbols. *Mala* is actually a ancient Sanskrit term meaning "garland."

Fig. A

PEACE SYMBOL
bracelet

BEADING SUPPLIES
60 round coral beads, 5mm
36 round mother of pearl beads, 5mm
1 silver lobster clasp
2 silver beads, 2mm
2 silver beads, 3mm
2 silver crimp beads
1 silver peace charm
1 silver jump ring
Beading thread

TOOLS &
OTHER SUPPLIES
Beading needle
Scissors

INSTRUCTIONS
Bracelet length: 8"

Start:
1. Thread a needle with 45" of beading thread. Thread a 3mm silver bead, 2mm silver bead, crimp bead, and one side of the lobster clasp on the thread about 3" from the end. Tie the clasp in place.
2. Thread the needle back through the crimp bead and both silver beads. Crimp bead.

String the beads:
1. Thread six coral beads on the needle and thread. Pass the needle back through the first four beads. Pull beads into a circle (Fig. A).
2. Thread two mother of pearl beads, two coral beads, and two mother of pearl beads on the needle and thread. Pass the needle back through the two previous coral beads (Fig. B). Pull the beads into a circle.
3. Thread four coral beads on the needle and thread. Pass the needle back through two previous coral beads (Fig. C). Pull the beads into a circle.
4. Thread two mother of pearl beads, two coral beads, and two mother of

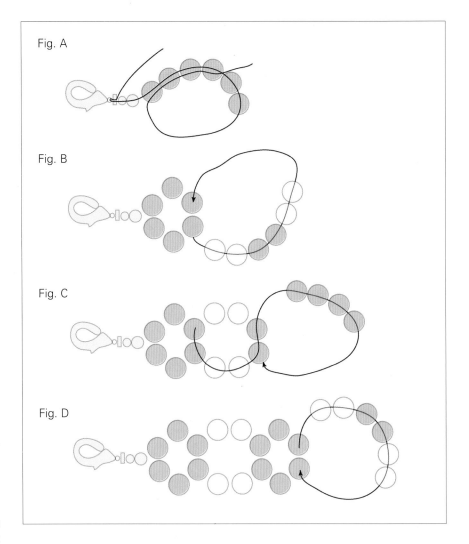

Fig. A

Fig. B

Fig. C

Fig. D

pearl beads on the needle and thread. Pass the needle back through two previous coral beads (Fig. D). Pull beads into a circle.
5. Continue adding beads (as shown in Figs. C and D) to make a length of 6-1/2". Pass the needle back through the last circle. Bring the needle out between the last two beads.

Finish:
1. Thread a 3mm silver bead, 2mm silver bead, crimp bead, and the other side of the clasp.
2. Knot the thread around the end of the clasp. Pass the needle back through the crimp bead and silver beads. Crimp bead.
3. Run the thread tail back through several beads. Thread the beginning thread tail on the needle. Pass the tail back through several beads. Trim the threads.
4. Attach the silver charm to one end of the bracelet with a jump ring. ❑

Coral and mother of pearl have peaceful, healing energies. They are combined in this bracelet and accented with a silver peace symbol charm.

Designed by Patty Cox

PRAYER BOX
sodalite necklace & earrings

Two forms of sodalite beads are used in this necklace, which holds a silver prayer box.
The three strands are held together by ornamental 3-into-1 silver connectors. Sodalite aids
in meditation and is a perfect bead to use in combination with a prayer box.

Designed by Patty Cox

BEADING SUPPLIES

120 (approx.) round sodalite beads, 4mm

20" strand of sodalite bead chips

Dark blue-gray seed beads

2 silver 3-into-1 connectors, 22x16mm

1 silver lobster clasp, 12mm

1 silver prayer box charm

2 silver 3-hole chandelier earring parts

2 silver ear wires

6 silver crimp beads

8 silver jump rings

6 silver eye pins

Beading wire, .014

TOOLS & OTHER SUPPLIES

Wire cutters

Crimping tool

Clamps *or* bead stoppers

Measuring tape

Masking tape

Roundnose pliers

About Prayer Boxes

Prayer boxes are containers for items of personal or religious significance. Using a prayer box typically involves writing a prayer on a tiny piece of paper and placing it in the box. They have been used by adherents of many faiths, including Hindus, Buddhists, Christians, Moslems, and Jews. Prayer boxes may be decorated with religious symbols, gemstones, or inspirational words.

Today prayer boxes are worn as jewelry by both religious and non-religious people. They may also be used to hold sentimental objects, such as lock of hair or a child's first tooth, or to hold an inspirational message written on a piece of paper, or for other secular uses, such as carrying medication, herbs, or aromatherapy botanicals.

INSTRUCTIONS
Necklace length: 17"

1. Cut three 24" lengths of beading wire. Thread a crimp bead on one wire. Thread the wire end through one of the loops in the 3-into-1 connector, then back through the crimp bead. Leave a 1" tail. Crimp bead. Repeat to connect all three wires.

2. Thread one outer wire with an 18" of sodalite bead chips. Clamp wire end, or thread a stop bead on wire while you string the other strands.

Photo 1 - The three strands on the 3-into-1 connector.

Continued on page 126

Continued from page 124

3. Thread middle wire with 18" of seed beads. Add the prayer box charm to the wire. Clamp wire end.

4. Thread the remaining outer wire with 18" of 4mm sodalite round beads, placing a seed bead between each sodalite bead. Clamp wire end. See Photo 1.

5. Measure to find the center point on the seed bead (middle) strand. Place a small piece of masking tape on the strand to mark the center.

6. Braid the three strands, beginning at the connector on the end. When you reach the tape marking the center of the middle strand, slide the prayer box charm to the center. Remove tape. Continue braiding the strands until you reach the ends of the beads.

7. Thread a crimp bead on one wire. Thread the wire end around one outer hole of the other 3-into-1 connector, then back through the crimp bead and several beads. Pull wire taut. Crimp bead. Cut wire tail. Repeat the process to connect the other three strands to the 3-into-1 connector.

8. Attach one part of the lobster clasp to each 3-into-1 connector.

EARRINGS

1. On a head pin, thread a seed bead, three 4mm sodalite round beads, and three seed beads. Cut the wire 3/8" from the last bead.

2. Form the head pin end into a loop, using roundnose pliers.

3. Attach the head pin to the chandelier earring part with a jump ring.

4. Make and attach two more beaded head pins.

5. Open the ear wire loop and attach to the earring part.

6. Repeat steps 1 through 5 to make the other earring. ❏

METRIC CONVERSION CHART

Inches to Millimeters and Centimeters

Inches	MM	CM	Inches	MM	CM
1/8	3	.3	2	51	5.1
1/4	6	.6	3	76	7.6
3/8	10	1.0	4	102	10.2
1/2	13	1.3	5	127	12.7
5/8	16	1.6	6	152	15.2
3/4	19	1.9	7	178	17.8
7/8	22	2.2	8	203	20.3
1	25	2.5	9	229	22.9
1-1/4	32	3.2	10	254	25.4
1-1/2	38	3.8	11	279	27.9
1-3/4	44	4.4	12	305	30.5

Yards to Meters

Yards	Meters	Yards	Meters
1/8	.11	3	2.74
1/4	.23	4	3.66
3/8	.34	5	4.57
1/2	.46	6	5.49
5/8	.57	7	6.40
3/4	.69	8	7.32
7/8	.80	9	8.23
1	.91	10	9.14
2	1.83		

INDEX

Continued on next page

INDEX